National Parks

By Matt and Karen Smith

We encourage and welcome your feedback.

Email us: dearbobandsue@gmail.com
Follow us on Facebook:
http://www.facebook.com/dearbobands
Visit our website: http://www.dearbobandsue.com

Disclaimer: This book reflects the opinions of the authors related to their experiences while traveling to the national parks. Some names and details of people and events were changed to protect individual's privacy.

Preface

We don't remember the moment or even the day we decided to visit all 58 national parks. But it called us just the same. We had spent the previous 28 years working and raising kids. Once they were grown and out of the house, we no longer needed to be home for them. It was time to take a break. The decisive factor may have been that we'd seen friends and family members, our age or younger, die before they did all the things they wanted.

So, in the spring of 2010, during the worst economy in our lifetime – with no guarantee we would find employment when we finished – we quit our jobs and began the journey.

Our interest in the national parks came from our dear friends, Bob and Sue. Their passion for the parks had begun before we met them. From the time their kids were babies, they spent most of their vacations visiting the parks. Their stories inspired us. We wish they had joined us on this adventure, but since they didn't we sent them updates on our progress with occasional e-mails, texts, phone calls and a couple of in-person visits. (They no longer live just down the street.)

In the fall of 2010, we began writing about our trip but were struggling with the tone and format for the book. It was then that I sent the Ahwahnee letter (dated September 14, 2010) to Bob and Sue along with *gifts* from our hotel room and Bob's pocketknife from Sequoia. I said to Karen, "I wish that writing the book were as easy as writing to Bob and Sue." That's when the idea came to us. We would write about our trip as a series of letters to Bob and Sue; later we changed the format to emails. (If we were 20 or 30 years younger, we would have written this book as a series of text messages.) In full disclosure, we didn't send all these emails to Bob and Sue on the dates indicated. But, they are real people; their names really are Bob and Sue, and the events we've written about actually happened.

This is not a guide to the national parks. We didn't have time to see everything we wanted in every park, and we know we missed a lot of great stuff. We didn't camp, rock climb, scuba dive or snorkel, but we did what we love: we hiked, drank beer and had the time of our lives. This is a series of snapshots and impressions based on our experience. We hope you enjoy reading it and are inspired to create your own memories in the national parks.

Matt and Karen Smith

Publishing note: *Dear Bob and Sue Volume One: Into the National Parks* covers our journey through the first 33 parks we visited.

From: **Matt Smith**
Subject: **We don't get these days back**
Date: **March 27, 2010**

Dear Bob and Sue,

    Karen and I are quitting our jobs and going to visit all the national parks. You guys should come with us.

Your Friend,
Matt

From: **Matt Smith**
Subject: **Mouse-on-head**
Date: **April 16, 2010**

Dear Bob and Sue,

Planning our parks trip is harder than I thought it would be. Karen refuses to stay at any place where there's a possibility she'll wake up in the middle of the night with a mouse on her head. She was reading a review for a motel in Utah where a woman described how she woke up to see a mouse on her husband's head. Now, before I book any room, Karen wants to check the online reviews. On top of the other logistical challenges with planning a 58-park trip, I have to wait for her to give me the all clear, that the place hasn't had any "mouse-on-head" reports, before I can book it.

It's surprising how many mouse complaints there are online. A lodge in one of the national parks had several mouse mentions in their reviews. The manager posted a response in the lodge's defense. He made the point that the lodge is in a national park where there's a greater chance that animals would be in or around the property. And, all the animals in the park are protected, including mice, so the lodge is limited in what they can do to prevent them from being in the rooms. They're only allowed to keep them out, not kill them.

I said to Karen, "Do you care what happens in our room when we're asleep? I'm sure there had been times when mice were in our hotel room at night, maybe even running across our bodies, and you didn't know it." This, I'll admit, was a poor choice of words. She pulled her shoulders close to her ears and shivered as if she'd stuck her tongue in a light socket.

I tried a softer approach. "Karen, Sweetie, you'll have to get used to roughing it a little. There might be rodents in our future."

I can't wait to see what she does when we see our first tarantula.

Your Friend,
Matt

Note to Reader: There's something you should know about Karen; she's not a fan of rodents. She didn't like them before, but after her close encounter with a squirrel a few years ago she wants nothing to do with them.

One spring day I was away on a business trip; Karen was home with the kids. It was a warm afternoon, and she was sitting with our son Matthew at the computer in my office. The kitchen door to the backyard was open. They were reviewing a homework project when they heard what sounded like fingernails scratching on the hardwood floors in the kitchen and then a thumping gallop from our cat Sox. An instant later a squirrel raced into the office with the cat at its heels. In a panic, Karen grabbed Matthew and the cat and ran out of the office slamming the door behind her.

Her plan was to leave the squirrel in my office and let me deal with it when I got home in a few days; the homework could wait. But 30 minutes and two glasses of Merlot later, Karen saw the flaw in her plan. She wasn't worried so much about the inconvenience to me as she was the possibility of the squirrel shredding everything in my office. Or worse, she feared the smell of dead squirrel; there was a decent chance her scream had given it a heart attack.

Luckily the window in my office was open that afternoon; the only problem, there was a screen in the window. Karen figured if she could remove the screen, the squirrel, if it was still alive, would find its way back to the great outdoors.

My office was on the first floor, so she was able to remove the screen easily from the outside. Standing in the backyard at a safe distance, she watched the open window, but no squirrel appeared. Venetian blinds were down covering the window opening. Karen thought, "If I just reach in and pull the cord on the blinds I can raise them enough for the little rodent to see his escape route."

Taking deep breaths while standing on the third rung of our stepladder, Karen thought through exactly what she had to do: raise the blinds with one hand, pull the cord with the other, lock it in place and get the hell out of there. No problem, the squirrel was no doubt cowering in the corner.

Not quite.

As soon as she raised the blinds, the squirrel – according to Karen who was the only witness – saw daylight and flew through the air landing on her head. Its toes were caught in Karen's long hair as it made a desperate attempt to free itself. Karen said, "It was running in place on top of my head." She fell off the ladder and ran screaming through the backyard with the squirrel stuck to her head. (I'm sure it was only a few seconds, but time does stand still when there's a squirrel on your head.) It eventually freed its claws, jumped off her head and ran off.

Sue was the first person Karen called after she calmed down enough to speak. They discussed the situation thoroughly and agreed that shampooing several times with Head and Shoulders, rubbing the tiny scratch marks on her scalp with alcohol and drinking the rest of the bottle of Merlot were the proper steps to prevent rabies. I was her second call.

Karen gave me a second-by-second recounting of the event, complete with sound effects and a graphic description of how the squirrel's toes felt as they dug into her scalp. Then she told me the whole thing was my fault because I wasn't home to protect the family when it happened. Apparently being away earning a living was not an acceptable excuse. She also said she learned a valuable lesson that day. "Not to leave the back door open?" I guessed. No, the lesson was that all squirrels are evil and out to get her. (She also decided that she doesn't like "any animal related to squirrels" - whatever that means.)

From: **Matt Smith**
Subject: **OC without the D**
Date: **April 30, 2010**

Dear Bob and Sue,

We're getting ready for our parks trip, so I made a list of things I need to have in my backpack. I like being prepared. Karen thinks I over prepare; she calls this my OCD. I correct her every time telling her, "I'm OC, without the D." (I do *not* have a disorder.)

Karen shouldn't complain; she benefits from my OC. When we're traveling and need a flashlight, I have one; when we need a bottle opener I have two. (I carry two in case I lose one. I hid a third in Karen's backpack just in case I lose both of mine.) There's no "D" and I wish she would stop saying it.

Today Karen saw the list on my dresser. I was trying to keep her from seeing it because she makes fun of my lists. With a straight face, she started to ask me a question about it, but before the question came out she looked like she was going to cry, and then covered her face with her hands. She laughed so hard she couldn't speak and walked out of the room. Ten minutes later she came back. As soon as she saw me: crying face, hands up, walked out of the room.

Why is this funny? We're going into the wilderness and need to be prepared. If I don't have a list I'll forget something, and then what? What if we need duct tape and don't have any? What would we do? Probably not survive that's what.

If she thinks I'm going to share my stuff with her when we're out in the wild she's mistaken. Maybe, if I need her body warmth, I'll barter.

I want to travel light, so I'm keeping my list to the bare minimum: emergency space blanket, zip lock bags, analog compass, sunglasses, binoculars, postcard stamps, sunscreen, chap stick with SPF 15 or higher, bug spray, Purell, bottle opener, Advil, liquid bandage, dental floss, finger and/or toenail clippers, reading glasses, peppermint patties, extra house keys,

30' section of nylon cord (I don't know why I need this, but it's on all the lists of things to have in case of an emergency), medical tape, wet wipes, extra flashlight batteries, napkins, water, snacks, GPS, extra batteries for the GPS, scissors, tweezers, tick remover, small roll of duct tape, Imodium A-D, small tripod, camera, backup bottle opener, knife, fire starter, bear spray, Spork (combination spoon/knife/fork), blister patch, gauze, earplugs, Dramamine and micro puff vest.

All that's in Karen's backpack is three used Kleenex, four and a half candy corns, a tampon, the bottle opener I hid in there and two Corona Light bottle caps. It's all a big joke until she needs something and doesn't have it. Then my OC isn't that funny. She better hope she doesn't need my Imodium A-D on our flight to American Samoa. I'm not sure I'll have any to spare.

Your friend,
Matt

From: **Matt Smith**
Subject: **Our national parks passport**
Date: **May 10, 2010**

Dear Bob and Sue,

It's a memorable moment when your spouse says, "You were right and I was wrong." I'm guessing of course because Karen has never said this.

I found her today admiring her national parks passport, the little blue book you introduced to us years ago. At first Karen laughed at the idea of a national parks passport, but now she's proud of hers. She can't wait to get a stamp from every national park.

I bought my passport in April 2006 at Grand Canyon National Park. When I was in the checkout line at the Grand Canyon bookstore I had asked Karen if she wanted me to buy her one. I had suggested to her that she start collecting park stamps with me on that trip. She gave me her best annoyed-to-have-to-answer-such-a-stupid-question look and said, "No thanks, I'm a grown up." For the last four years, I've endured her rolling of eyes whenever I would hunt for the stamp at a national park. All the while I was accumulating an impressive collection.

Then it happened, as I knew it would someday. It was earlier this year, and we were packing for a trip to Tucson. Karen said to me, "Don't forget our national parks passport." I paused for effect then replied, "*Our* passport? (pause again) Sweetie, *we* don't have a passport. *I* have a passport."

She tried to get me to acknowledge that it was now *our* passport, even using her "everything we have belongs to both of us because we are companions-for-life and so much in love, yada, yada, yada" line. Shameless. I didn't give in.

On that trip, she bought her very own passport at Saguaro National Park. She carries it with her everywhere, and if anyone asks, will show it with pride. Now she wishes she had it all those times we visited national parks before. I guess I was right. At least she has one now - with fewer stamps than me.

Your Friend,
Matt

From: **Matt Smith**
Subject: **#1 – North Cascades National Park**
Date: **June 6, 2010**

Dear Bob and Sue,

I sneezed, and Karen jumped three feet in the air. Our rattlesnake talk with the ranger spooked her. It was a beautiful hike along Lakeshore Trail in Stehekin, but Karen was walking with her head down, scanning for snakes and listening for rattles. Earlier in the day (Friday) at the Golden West Visitor Center, we asked a ranger for afternoon hiking suggestions and she recommended this hike. Her only warning, "Watch out for rattlesnakes sleeping in the sun on the trail."

She went on to tell us, "If they bite you, they probably won't use their venom. They can sense you're too big to eat by the vibrations you make when you walk, so they won't waste their venom on you." I wasn't comforted by this; it was like someone telling me that they're going to shoot me in the calf with a nail gun, but don't worry, the nails are clean. Karen wasn't comforted either. She said she wanted to see the ranger's diploma from snake school.

Whenever we hike in an area with rattlesnakes, Karen has a scenario running through her head where a rattlesnake strikes from out of nowhere and sinks its fangs into her leg. I make an incision with my pocketknife just above the bite, suck out the venom before it reaches her heart and save her life. What she fails to realize is by the time I found my pocketknife, sharpened it with my honing stone and sterilized it and the bite area with my travel size alcohol wipes, the venom would have done its damage. Fortunately, we had the trail to ourselves – no snakes and few people.

North Cascades National Park – in northwest Washington State – is an area of remote mountains, deep valleys and more than 300 glaciers. And it's difficult to reach. Looking at a map, I couldn't find a road we could drive into the park. The National

Park Service manages North Cascades National Park, Ross Lake National Recreation Area and Lake Chelan National Recreation Area as a single park unit. We'd always wanted to stay at the lodge in Stehekin (in Lake Chelan NRA), and we thought we could hike or bike into the park from there. That's why we went to Stehekin this weekend.

Three of the kids went with us – Rachel, her husband Justin and Matthew – Emily is home studying for finals (so she says). We're glad the kids joined us on our first park trip, but just Karen and I will be going to the other 57.

Lake Chelan is long and skinny, 51 miles in length and only a couple miles at its widest point. At the south end of the lake is the city of Chelan, a popular summer recreation spot. At the north end, where the Stehekin River dumps into Lake Chelan, sits the town of Stehekin, an isolated community tucked into a deep valley at the edge of the wilderness.

Stehekin is a native word for "the way through." The valley was once on the route the Indians used to cross over the Cascade Mountains, so they could trade with people to the west. Today it's not on route to anywhere; it's a dead end. The only way to get to Stehekin is by boat, floatplane or trail. There's a 23-mile road in the valley that is mostly gravel. Locals can arrange to have their vehicles put on a barge that runs every few weeks if they need them brought from or taken to Chelan.

Thursday night we drove from our home in Issaquah (Issaquah, Washington is 15 miles east of Seattle) to Chelan where we spent the night.

At 8:30am Friday morning we took the two and a half hour Lady of the Lake ferry from Chelan to Stehekin. As we traveled up the lake the surrounding hills gradually increased in elevation. Near Chelan the hills are low and gently rolling; in the summer, they're the color of straw except for the neatly spaced lines of green made by the irrigated orchards and vineyards. At Stehekin, the peaks are more than 7,000 feet and rise nearly vertical out of the 1,486-foot deep lake. By the time the boat docked, we felt we were in a different world than the one we had come from only a few hours before.

There was time to kill before we could check into our cabin, so we walked the mile and a half to the valley bakery for lunch. Stehekin has fewer than 100 year-round residents; it's not a crowded place. While we were walking, four different people in pickup trucks stopped and asked if we wanted a ride. Normally we wouldn't consider taking a ride from a stranger, but here it's what people do; the residents all know one another and treat visitors like neighbors. It's an exceptionally safe place. We declined the offers, not out of concern, because we needed to stretch our legs after the long boat ride.

Lunch at the bakery was fantastic: chili, huge deli sandwiches and fresh baked cookies. Afterward, we walked back and checked into our cabin at the Stehekin Landing Resort, which sits right on the water by the ferry dock. Our cabin didn't have air-conditioning, TV, Internet or cell-phone service, but it had electricity, hot water, coffee maker and a magnificent view of the lake. After our Lakeshore Trail hike, we had dinner with the kids at the resort's restaurant, and again, the food was excellent. Stehekin may be remote, but they eat well.

Yesterday (Saturday) Karen and I got out of bed about 7am; we knew we had several hours to ourselves before there would be any sign of life from the other three. It was a beautiful morning, so we walked along the valley road. We could smell the bakery before we could see it; we had a relaxed breakfast of coffee and a shared cinnamon roll the size of a football.

At mid-morning, the five of us rented bikes at a stand across the road from the resort. We planned on riding along the valley road toward the park boundary. I asked the woman renting us the bikes if she had locks for us to use. She laughed and said, "We don't need locks here. No one's going to take your bike. If they do, they'll bring it back."

Our first stop along the valley road was the old Stehekin one-room schoolhouse. It was built in 1921 and used until the community built the new school in 1988. A short distance from the schoolhouse is Rainbow Falls where we had lunch at a Paul Bunyan sized picnic table within mist range of the 312-foot falls.

After lunch, we left our bikes in the grass alongside the valley road across from the falls, and walked to the 50-acre historic Buckner Orchard. The ranger at the visitor center made a point of telling us that *we* own Buckner Orchard since it's part of the park system, so we thought the least we could do is check it out and see how *our* orchard was doing. From the valley road a half-mile away, a hand dug irrigation ditch diverted water into the orchard from Boulder Creek just below Rainbow Falls. Water ran swiftly through the 100-year old ditch as if the Buckners had dug it only a few years ago.

The 1910 census recorded 13 people living in the Stehekin Valley. That was the year William Buckner bought the land that became the orchard. The Buckners – William, his wife Mae and their three sons – lived on the property during the summers until 1924. After that, one of the sons, Harry, continued to live there until 1970 when he sold the majority of the farm to the National Park Service. Now, some of the park service employees live there.

The ranger said the public may pick apples for free in the fall. For those who want to make cider, there's a hand crank contraption for grinding and pressing the apples. Karen says we're coming back in the fall to pick apples, and she's going to bake with them: apple pie, apple crisp, apple cobbler, Brown Betty. It's our first national park, and we're already planning a return trip. I'm not sure Karen gets it that we have to go back to work someday.

Our day of biking in the valley was perfect – sunny and temperature in the 70's – it was like riding a bike through a postcard. Just one problem, we didn't make it to the North Cascades National Park border. After all our side trips, we didn't have the energy to bike the remaining miles to the boundary. (We also weren't sure exactly where the boundary was.) I don't think we can count this as an official park visit.

This morning (Sunday) we woke up to the sound of rain on the metal roof of our cabin. Fortunately, we hadn't planned on doing much today except taking the ferry back to Chelan and driving home. Our butts were sore from yesterday's bike ride, and the rain was making it hard to get out of bed to pack for home.

Sitting inside the Lady of the Lake ferry, on our return trip to Chelan, there wasn't much conversation. I was trying to stay awake, but the rain and the sound of the boat's engine were making me sleepy. After a long silence Karen said, "Justin, I've been meaning to tell you about an article I read this week about the dangers of using a laptop. Researchers think that men who use a laptop while it's resting on their lap can damage their sperm. The laptop can cook their testicles. You don't use your laptop while it's on your lap do you?"

Justin looked terrified, so I jumped in to rescue him. "Karen, first, please don't use the phrase 'cook your testicles' *ever* again. Second, Justin doesn't want to talk about his testicles or his sperm with his mother-in-law."

"I'm serious." She continued, "It can cook his testicles. We want to have grandchildren someday." I put an end to the testicle discussion, but we couldn't find Justin for a long time after that.

We made it home safely; it was a fantastic trip but a false start to our parks trip, we still have 58 to go. I'm happy the kids came with us, but I think they've had enough of us for a while. Justin didn't say much on the drive home.

Your Friend,
Matt

From: **Matt Smith**
Subject: **It's blinking!**
Date: **June 10, 2010**

Dear Bob and Sue,

Today we hiked into North Cascades National Park, so we could claim that we officially visited the park. We found a spot along Highway 20 in northern Washington where we parked and hiked the few miles to the park boundary. On our way to the trailhead, we stopped to take our picture in front of the park sign in Sedro-Woolley – the park headquarters. We've added this to the list of things we plan on doing in every park.

We parked close to the sign, so I could balance my digital camera on the hood of the car. I set the timer for ten seconds, giving me enough time to get in position for the picture. There's a light on the front of the camera that starts blinking once the timer is set. When I pressed the button to start the timer Karen yelled, "It's blinking!" She scared the shit out of me. I thought someone threw a hand grenade at us. She says this every time we take a picture with the timer. Even after I've explained that I know when it is blinking because I'm the one pushing the button that is making it blink, she still yells, "It's blinking!"

The picture came out slanted because of the slope of the car's hood; I tried setting the camera on the ground. The perspective from down there made us look like giants in the picture. I found a box of saltines in the car and put the camera on the box. This was a slight improvement.

At first we were embarrassed about posing for our picture in front of the park sign. We waited until no one was around, but after a few takes, we stopped caring. People in passing cars would honk and shout at us, usually compliments such as, "Nice cracker box!"

It took many tries to get the picture just right. Karen didn't know what to do with her hands. At first she put them in front of her about waist high, limp at the wrist. I called this her squirrel pose. She insisted she was not holding her hands like a squirrel until I showed her the picture. We tried again. I ran back from the camera after setting the timer and said in a soft voice, "No squirrel" just before the flash went off.

Drawing attention to her squirrel pose made it harder for her not to hold her hands that way. On the second picture, she had one hand in squirrel position. Half-squirrel. On the third picture, she put her hands straight down at her sides as if she was jumping off a diving board. I called this the high-dive. Naming the poses made matters worse.

After each take, I would go back to the camera, and Karen would stay in position next to the sign. While I checked the picture Karen would yell, "Is it OK?" and I would yell back, "Full squirrel again," or "High dive," reset the camera and run back. Eventually we were laughing so hard that the picture came out perfect.

Your Friend,
Matt

From: **Karen Smith**
Subject: **#2 – Olympic National Park**
Date: **June 23, 2010**

Dear Bob and Sue,

Greetings from Lake Crescent Lodge on Washington's Olympic Peninsula. Matt and I have been staying here for the last two nights while visiting Olympic National Park. We reserved one of the Singer Tavern Cottages along the lake weeks ago. Yesterday, on our way to check-in at the main lodge, we were walking past the cottages when Matt pointed out that one of them was in an odd spot. It didn't face the lake; it faced the other cottages. Guess which one we got?

For about an hour after checking in, it was eating at him that we got the dud cabin. When he couldn't stand it any longer, we went to the lodge, and Matt asked the manager if we could move to another cottage. I went over to sit by the fireplace, acting like we weren't together, but I could still hear their conversation. The manager told Matt that all the other cottages were taken. He tried to smooth it over by saying we were *lucky* because our cottage was "one of the most requested cottages at the lodge." When I heard that I thought, "Uh oh." Matt has a low tolerance for bullshit (as if you didn't already know). He couldn't let that slide, "So, let me get this straight. What you're telling me is, that when people call to reserve a cottage, they say, 'I want the cottage that *doesn't* face the lake. I don't want any of the other cottages - the ones with a lake view. I want the cottage *without* the lake view.' Is this what you're telling me?" I let Matt go on for a couple of minutes, then went to the front desk and said, "I'm sorry to interrupt, but is it OK if we take our beers outside to the lawn by the lake?" Matt knew my interruption was code for, "stop being an asshole, you're only going to piss him off."

Olympic National Park has three completely different ecosystems: mountains, rainforest and ocean beach. We saw some of each on this visit. After our westbound ferry ride across

Puget Sound, we drove to Port Angeles, and then south to Hurricane Ridge inside the park. Two miles into the 17-mile road to the top, Matt ran over a chipmunk; he felt bad about it. He used to swerve to avoid hitting small wildlife, but I've complained many times – my face plastered to the windshield – that he's going to kill us trying to save a rodent. So, we now have a "no swerve" policy for any animal less than two pounds (kittens and puppies excluded). The chipmunk's death was not entirely Matt's fault though; it froze in the middle of the road. We went right over the top of him. Indecision in the wild is deadly.

We stopped at the Hurricane Ridge Visitor Center, stamped our passports, and took pictures of the amazing view from the back patio. The road beyond the visitor center was free of snow, so we drove to Hurricane Hill trailhead, parked, and hiked the easy three-mile round-trip trail. About a mile into the hike, we came across a scraggly old marmot; by the look of his fur, he'd seen one too many winters in the Olympic Mountains. Matt was very excited about this rare wildlife sighting until, farther up the trail, we came across many more. The trail was thick with marmots. At first Matt kept his distance; he was not sure if they were biters, but after seeing other hikers casually walk past them, he became more comfortable. Soon he was right in their faces taking pictures. They didn't move; these marmots were accustomed to hikers and cameras. Seeing so many close to the trail creeped me out, they're like giant squirrels. I never made eye contact with them, but I could still feel their beady little eyes following me.

After the hike, we drove to Lake Crescent Lodge, checked in and made friends with the manager. Then we relaxed in Adirondack chairs at the edge of the lake with a beer. Several beers. We may have napped. Eventually, we dragged our cooler into the lobby/bar area and found comfortable chairs close to the fireplace. We had discovered on a trip to Crater Lake Lodge last year that you can bring your own food and beverages into the lobbies of the national park lodges, even if you are not staying there.

When it was time for dinner, we decided to stay and eat in the bar area instead of the dining room. We ordered hamburgers, and after waiting for about a half an hour, we saw a kitchen worker bring out our hamburgers and leave them at the end of the bar. From across the room, we watched our hamburgers sit at the end of the bar. About five minutes later, we saw the bartender look at our hamburgers, say something to our waitress and shrug his shoulders. We then watched the bartender and waitress eat our hamburgers. I gave Matt a look with a raised eyebrow as if to say, "This is what happens when you piss them off." It took another half an hour, and several confused conversations with our waitress, to get new hamburgers. We keep reminding ourselves that staying in the national park lodges is about the park experience and not the food or the service.

The lodge was crowded with people who had returned from their day of activities in the park. They milled about while waiting for tables to open in the dining room. We could see them eyeing us, wondering how we got the comfortable chairs next to the fire, and if we were leaving any time soon. There was no way we were giving up our prime real estate. We sat there and read for a couple of hours. The front doors of the lodge were open and a small red squirrel kept running into the great room; his little toenails made a skidding/scratching sound as he raced from place to place. I couldn't stand it, so I read with my feet on top of the cooler.

Close by, two couples sat on couches while they waited for their table. They were talking about all the parks they had been to, national parks and others. Their list was impressive. It made me realize we're novices, this being the second park of our trip. One of the men said, "I don't know what it is, but when I see those brown park signs my heart beats a little faster." It's interesting to see other people drawn to the parks, like Matt and I, without being able to explain it.

This morning we drank our coffee while gazing out the window of our cottage at the reflection of the lake in the windows of the other cottages. We were up and out early; the drive from the lodge to the Hoh Rain Forest Visitor Center took nearly two hours. We hiked the Hall of Mosses Loop, and then a several mile section the Hoh River Trail. I love rainforests. With all the draping, dripping moss, this one looked like an enchanted forest straight out of a storybook.

We didn't bring lunch with us, so we backtracked to the town of Forks and ate at Sully's Drive Inn. Sully's is an old dairy freeze style hamburger place. The area in front of the walk-up order window was enclosed – it looked like it had originally been open to the outside – and had several booths to sit at and eat. There was a weird mix of customers having lunch; everyone in their own way looked out of place: loggers in their canvas overalls, three college students with laptops and University of Washington t-shirts - their car overflowing with camping equipment - several pairs of Goth looking tourists, and us in our hiking clothes.

In Forks, we saw several tour buses. These buses were not taking people into Olympic National Park; they were touring the town. Since you have a teenager, you probably know that the Twilight vampire books and movies are set in Forks. It seems odd that people would pay money to tour places where fictional characters hang out. It's all made up. They didn't even film the movies in Forks.

After lunch, we headed to the Pacific Coast; much of the Pacific coastline on the Olympic Peninsula is part of the park. We drove to a parking lot adjacent to Rialto Beach and walked along the beach to the Hole-in-the-Wall. It was cold and windy, and the spray off the high waves made us damp. There were interesting pieces of driftwood everywhere; even wood that might have been construction debris – small lengths of two by four – had been rounded smooth as if they'd spent a month in a giant rock tumbler. I found a piece of driftwood that looked like a dinosaur with a long neck, and was going to bring it home until Matt said it looked like a giant penis. I was about to disagree with him when he held out his camera and showed me the picture of me holding it tightly by the neck with a stupid grin on my face. I immediately dropped it on the beach. It's just as well, you're not supposed to remove anything from a national park anyway.

Right now we're back in the Lake Crescent Lodge bar again, having a beer and wishing you were here. We just ordered hamburgers. It looks like a different bartender tonight. Hopefully, he's already had dinner.

Your friend,
Karen

From: **Matt Smith**
Subject: **#3 – Mount Rainier National Park**
Date: **June 30, 2010**

Dear Bob and Sue,

I learned during our visit to Mount Rainier National Park that to impersonate a national park ranger is against the law. Last night, we stayed at Paradise Inn, inside the park on the south side of the mountain. Before leaving the lodge this morning, I asked a park ranger how one would go about getting an official park ranger uniform. We thought it would be a nice birthday gift for you, Bob. I can see you now in the dark green wool trousers; the straw hat with the pinecone embossed leather band and a bear spray holster loaded and ready. You could wear the uniform in your back yard, and practice for when you retire and become a park ranger. When friends come over, you could rope off rooms in your house and give make-believe tours as if it was Harry Truman's house. Or, you could wear it on the weekends when you go to the Home Depot to get a bag of nails, or whatever it is you get there.

The ranger seemed concerned that I was trying to get an official uniform. She said something about it being a federal offense to impersonate a park ranger. I can't imagine this is a big problem for the National Park Service, fake rangers leading unauthorized interpretive hikes. Regardless, keep this in mind if you're planning on going out in public in the ranger uniform I'm going to find for you.

I hadn't gotten off to a good start with this ranger. I told her about our plan to visit all 58 national parks. She said, "You know there are more than 58 national parks, don't you?" I acknowledged that there were 300+ park units, but told her that we had decided to go to only the 58 that were named *national park*. She didn't seem too happy that we were placing a higher priority on some of the park units than others; she was a bit... severe. She then asked, "How many parks have you been to so far?" When I told her that Mount Rainier was our third, she smiled and said "Good luck."

Mount Rainier National Park is a two-hour drive southeast of Seattle, Washington. It was made the 5th national park in 1899 to preserve the wilderness around the volcano: the old growth forests and the sub-alpine wildflower meadows. The centerpiece of the park is the massive 14,410-foot volcanic peak of Mount Rainier; its year-round, glacier covered peak is nature's lighthouse for the entire Pacific Northwest. It has the highest topographic prominence of any mountain in the lower 48 states. This means it looks taller than mountains its same size because the land that surrounds it is so much lower in elevation. Sea level is only 50 miles away.

On a clear day, we can see Mount Rainier from our hometown of Issaquah. For years, I've thought about climbing it, but Karen discouraged me. She thinks it's dangerous. She also didn't want to raise three kids by herself; I can't blame her.

Over the last 30 years, there have been an average of two deaths per year of people climbing Mount Rainier; an unfortunate number, but a small percentage of those who try. In 1966, the number of climbers attempting the summit was 2,000. By 1994, the number had grown to 10,000. It's stayed close to that level ever since. During the 2009 climbing season (October 2008 – September 2009), 10,616 climbers took a shot at it; about half succeeded in reaching the summit.

By far the most popular routes to the summit start at the Henry M. Jackson Memorial Visitor Center parking lot (adjacent to the Paradise Inn). Most climbers hike from the visitor center to Camp Muir – about a 5,000-foot vertical climb – spend the night, and start an early morning push to the summit, which is another 4,000 vertical feet. Most climbers, whether they are successful at summiting or not, make it down without injury or the need for rescue or assistance. The reason for this is that almost half of the climbers use one of the three professional guide companies licensed by the park service.

Last year there were 18 climbing related search and rescue incidents in the park: climbers breaking bones (ankles, legs, ribs, pelvis), one climber was hit in the face with a rock and lost consciousness, several suffered acute mountain sickness (headache, nausea, dizziness), and one incident involved a ranger who fell 30 feet into a crevasse after accidentally skiing into it. He was lucky to have survived.

Karen and I didn't attempt to climb Mount Rainier on this trip; we settled for hiking in the forests in the lower regions of the park. With all the attention on the summit, the trails through the old growth forests are nearly deserted. The park service issues more permits for climbing the summit than for overnight backpacking in the entire rest of the park. That's quite amazing since the park is 368 square miles.

Yesterday, when we got here, we entered through the Stevens Canyon Entrance in the southeast corner of the park. The trailhead for the Grove of the Patriarchs Trail is just inside the park. The grove is made up of Western Hemlock, Douglas fir, and Western red cedar trees. Some are more than one thousand years old. We hiked the short loop to the patriarchs, and then continued hiking several miles north along the Ohanapecosh River.

A couple of miles into the hike, we met park workers who were building bridges with blown down trees. They were improving the trail enough to get tools and stock to a river crossing farther north where they needed to prepare footings for a steel span bridge being delivered by helicopter later this summer. It looked like a fun job, chain saws, hard hats, large trees attached to steel cables being winched into place. I could easily imagine them being a CCC (Civilian Conservation Corps) crew from the 1930's. The lead ranger said the CCC built some of the bridges they were replacing. He told us of a bridge farther up the trail that the CCC built in the 1930's that's still in excellent shape. The original square head nails they used on the planks, now smooth from the better part of a century of hiking boots passing over them, are still visible.

After leaving the bridge builders, we hiked to the river crossing they had told us about where the steel span bridge was to go. The existing bridge was a single log stretching 30 feet across the Ohanapecosh River at a point where the river drops about 100 feet. The falls were beautiful, but I was nervous walking across the log. One misplaced step would have ended of our parks trip.

I videotaped Karen as she walked slowly across the log, looking down and carefully putting one foot in front of the other. She accused me of doing this so, if she had fallen I'd have proof I didn't push her. I was deeply offended.

After our hike, we drove to Paradise Inn. The inn, at 5,400 feet elevation, opened in 1917. There have been several attempts over the years to make Paradise a recreation destination; they built a golf course and towrope for skiing, but those are gone now – they weren't economically sustainable. Today the main activity is hiking and climbing.

Paradise Inn has been remodeled several times; the most recent project was a two-year renovation from mid-2006 to mid-2008 when the inn was reinforced to be able to withstand a major earthquake. Mount Rainier is an active volcano, and, in an average month, there are several small earthquakes on the mountain. There are seismic sensors on the mountain, and scientists believe that if (or when) it erupts, there will be enough warning to evacuate visitors from the park safely. But you never know. Even though the last major eruption was in the mid-nineteenth century, Mount Rainier is one of the most dangerous volcanoes in the world because of how close it is to the Seattle-Tacoma metropolitan area. If Mount Rainier blows in the direction of our house in Issaquah, well, let's just say the park would be visiting us – in a hurry.

We had wanted to stay at Paradise Inn since it re-opened in 2008; our parks trip was a good excuse to do it. Last night, we sat in the great room for hours reading and writing postcards. Karen is sending a postcard to each of our kids from every national park we visit. After 58 parks, they will each have a complete set of postcards. Wow! What 20-something year-old wouldn't want a postcard from all 58 national parks?

This morning, there was still five feet of snow next to the road leading away from the inn; the snowpack is 200 percent of normal for this time of the year. Driving down the mountain, there was a mile long section of the road where we saw several marmots. They were odd looking, as if they were made from marmot spare parts. They have a blond nose and midsection, but they have a black head. Then, the back third of their body is light brown. They were Hoary Marmots, which are different from the Olympic Marmots we saw in Olympic National Park. Marmots prefer a very narrow band of elevation; that's why we saw so many in one place on our hike in Olympic, and why we saw so many in one place along the road this morning.

Before heading for home, we hiked several miles of the Wonderland Trail, a 93-mile path that circumnavigates Mount Rainier. About 250 people each year hike the entire trail, which takes an average of 14 days to complete. The park service requires a permit to hike the entire trail. They want to keep track of the backcountry hikers and to ensure the backcountry campsites aren't overcrowded. In November 2006, a storm caused flooding that took out most of the trail's log bridge creek crossings; it was August 2007 before the trail re-opened. Ironically, people who have hiked the Wonderland Trail say that even though the trail circles the mountain, the mountain is rarely visible from the trail. The section we hiked was relatively easy, the elevation gains were small, and for most of it, the trail followed Stevens Creek through a valley south of the main park road.

We're lucky that three of the national parks are a short drive from our house; we've made a good start without even leaving Washington. But, the ones close to home are over now. Next week we start traveling farther; we'll be visiting Cuyahoga Valley National Park in Ohio.

Your Friend,
Matt

From: **Karen Smith**
Subject: **#4 – Cuyahoga Valley National Park**
Date: **July 6, 2010**

Dear Bob and Sue,

Before planning our parks trip, we'd never heard of Cuyahoga Valley National Park. Just south of Cleveland, it includes 33,000 acres along 22 miles of the Cuyahoga River. The river is the most famous part of the park – for being polluted. So polluted, it caught fire *at least 13 times* between 1868 and 1969. But the health of the river is improving, and while the National Park Service hasn't prohibited recreational activities in the river, they seriously discourage them. The park newsletter warns that the river is contaminated with pathogens such as E. coli. Signs are posted that say "No Swimming, No Wading, No Boating." We didn't need signs to keep us away – they had us at E. coli.

We got to the park yesterday just after noon. It was warm and humid, even for July. Our first stop was the Canal Visitor Center, on the north end of the park, where we stamped our passports and looked around the museum. Anxious to see the park, we drove south to Hunt Farm Visitor Center, stopping at the two other visitor centers along the way. Immediately, we noticed the park didn't have the "you've entered a sacred, pristine place" feeling that we get in the other national parks. It was a hodgepodge of forest, houses, small businesses and highways crisscrossing overhead. The road we drove through the park, Canal Road, unexpectedly changed names, took us out of the park and changed names again. There were so many roads in and out of the park that we were never sure when we were in the park and when we weren't. It felt like a typical rural area in the Midwest rather than a national park.

We knew, before we got here, that Cuyahoga Valley National Park was different from the other national parks. It didn't become a national park to protect a rare or unusual landscape or other natural resource. It became a national park because the local citizens wanted it to be a national park. By the

1960's, the valley was in danger of becoming an unbroken chain of urban development from Cleveland to Akron. Local leaders decided it needed the protection that a National Park Service site is assured.

The park service and Department of the Interior resisted, not wanting to divert funds from the western *crown jewel* parks like Yellowstone and Yosemite. In 1973, the National Park Service director declared, "I will tell you one thing. (The Cuyahoga Valley) will be a park over my dead body!" The following year, President Ford, under pressure from environmental groups, reluctantly signed the bill that established Cuyahoga Valley National Recreation Area.

Over the following 34 years, more than $200 million was spent to purchase land for the park, restore nearly 100 historic structures and establish activities for visitors. Eventually, supporters called for full national *park* status, and they got it. In 2000, the name was changed to Cuyahoga Valley National Park. In a nutshell, locals got the federal government to purchase and restore their polluted landscape, manage these outdoor spaces and provide recreation and cultural activities for the millions of people living just outside its borders.

One activity we had been looking forward to doing was riding the Cuyahoga Valley Scenic Railroad. It's "one of the oldest, longest, and most scenic tourist excursion railways in the country, running 51 miles from Independence, Ohio through the park and continuing to Akron and Canton." You can board the train at the north end of the park, – at Rockside Station – get off at stops throughout the park, and re-board later for the return trip. But, when we asked a ranger about the train, he told us that it doesn't run on Mondays or Tuesdays (the only days we're here).

Since we had planned a whole day around riding the train, we found ourselves with time to fill. We asked the rangers for recommendations of things to do. One of them suggested we go to the beaver marsh at dawn or dusk to see beaver activity. They are understandably proud of their beaver activity, because, by 1900, there were almost no beavers left in the Cuyahoga Valley due to unrestricted hunting. The ranger told us beavers created a marsh on top of what was previously an automobile junkyard. We were expecting to hear a feel-good story about how the park service removed the trash and restored the area to its natural state, but the beavers moved too quickly. They took matters into their own paws, dammed the stream and created a marsh right on top of the junked cars.

Today instead of riding the train, we hiked to Bradywine Falls and then the Ledges and Pine Grove trails. It was hot and humid again, temps in the 90's. The Ledges Trail is any easy 2.2-mile loop through a hemlock forest that passes by several 30-60 foot tall sandstone cliffs (the ledges). It also goes by Ice Box Cave, which isn't a real cave but a 50-foot deep, narrow slit in the rock hillside. At the entrance, we felt cold air coming out of the cave. It would have been the perfect day to sit inside. I peered into the darkness.

"Let's go in and take a look around," I said to Matt. "Do you have a flashlight?" Matt shrugged his shoulders. He hates caves. "I know you have a flashlight. For God's sake, you have everything from batteries to a tick remover. Surely you have a flashlight."

He replied, "Do you have a tick that needs removing?"

"Come on. You could supply a medical clinic with what you have in your backpack. Do you really expect me to believe you don't have a flashlight?"

He said, "Look, it would be easy to hand you my flashlight, but then you wouldn't have learned anything. We're in a national park; you need to work on your survival skills. Take those two Corona Light bottle caps out of your backpack and try rubbing them together to get a spark. Use your dirty Kleenex as kindling." Matt never wastes an opportunity to point out my lack of preparation.

Just then, 20 kids – who looked to be fourth graders – arrived and swarmed the area in and around the cave. One of them ran right into Matt, got behind him, and grabbed Matt's legs. He was hiding from his friends behind Matt like Matt was a tree. The kid peeked around Matt's backpack then ran away with a squeal. Matt was momentarily trapped in the scrum of children. I continued down the trail, "See ya back at the car, honey."

We had thought about renting bikes and then riding along the Towpath trail, but it was too hot. The Towpath Trail is the same path that mules once walked on while towing canal boats along the Ohio and Erie Canal. In the 1820's, the 308-mile waterway was built to carry freight, but the railroads later made the canal obsolete. By 1913, much of the canal was abandoned, which explains why the part of the canal we saw looked like a ditch choked with weeds. It's hard to imagine boats filled with cargo ever using this as a means of transportation, but they did, and local citizens wanted protection for the sections of the canal outside of what was then the National Recreation Area.

In 1996, Congress designated The Ohio and Erie Canalway a National Heritage Area to preserve the canal, and everything surrounding the first 110 miles of it: rails, trails, landscapes and towns. They rebuilt 81 miles of the Towpath Trail following most of the original Towpath route by using historic maps and remnants of the trail itself. Twenty miles of the trail run though the park, and it's usually crowded with walkers, runners, strollers and bicyclists – more than 2.5 million people annually – but very few of them were out today.

We went to the Winking Lizard Tavern in Peninsula, Ohio, a small historic town in the middle of the park. Between yesterday and today, we've been there three times. They're currently hosting their 24th annual World Tour of Beers. A Tour Card electronically keeps track of the beers you've consumed, and when you've had 100 beers from their World Tour of Beers list, you receive the coveted World Tour jacket. If we were spending a few more days in the park, we'd wear our World Tour jackets back to Seattle, but tomorrow we're heading home.

Your Friend,
Karen

From: **Karen Smith**
Subject: **Princess and the pea**
Date: **July 9, 2010**

Dear Sue,

I'm seriously considering eating the expired marshmallow fluff that's been in the back of our pantry since Christmas. That's how bad today's been. I had my annual checkup with my OB/GYN. Usually the appointment is very quick, and I'm in and out in 15 minutes, like the express lube lane at the dealership. I get a postcard every year when it's time to schedule my next service appointment. Today was different.

After reviewing my chart, my doctor asked me how Alison was doing and was shocked when I told her that she died last August. She wanted to know if Alison had ever been tested for the BRCA gene mutation. (She had not.) If you're unfamiliar with BRCA1 and BRCA2 genes: in normal cells they help prevent uncontrolled cell growth, but the mutation of these genes is linked to hereditary breast and ovarian cancer. The doctor said that based on my sister's and my dad's cancers, there's a high chance this gene mutation runs in our family. If I've inherited it, I would be five times more likely to develop breast cancer and ten to thirty times more likely to develop ovarian cancer. There would also be a 50 percent chance that I passed the gene mutation on to my girls. She strongly encouraged me to get tested. Of course, I will.

After that depressing conversation, things got worse. During the breast exam, the doctor found a lump. Left side. Size of a pea. I was so shocked that I said the first stupid thing that came into my head, "OK, thanks for letting me know. I'll make sure and mention it next month when I have my annual mammogram."

She shook her head. "No, this needs to be looked at **immediately.**" She wasn't kidding around. I got a call from the hospital's Breast Diagnostic Center before I even left the building. My appointment is Monday morning. It's scary when they get you in that fast. They'll do a mammogram, a sonogram and possibly an MRI; then a doctor will look at the images immediately while we wait and then tell us the results.

So I'm kind of freaking out. We've made big plans. We quit our jobs. I have a shiny new national parks passport with just a handful of stamps in it, three of which are from parks in our back yard. I want to see a grizzly bear, a moose, a glacier, a cave, an erupting volcano and the northern lights. I know I shouldn't be thinking the worst, but what if we waited too long?

It's ironic, isn't it? If I learned anything from my sister's death, it's that life is unpredictable. There are no guarantees that any of us will be here tomorrow. That was the main reason we decided to do our parks trip now. That, and I really want to see a bear.

Sorry for putting all this is an email, but I was pretty sure if I heard your voice I would cry. I need to pull myself together and scrounge something up for dinner. Matt said the best distraction would be to continue all my normal activities, like cooking and cleaning. He was kidding, of course. He's been really great about all this. You would be proud of him.

Love you lots.

Wish you were here to hold my hand,
Karen

From: **Karen Smith**
Subject: **Pig-in-a blanket**
Date: **July 12, 2010**

Dear Sue,

Matt and I decided over the weekend that if this pea turns out to be nothing, we're driving straight from the hospital to IHOP, and ordering as many pancakes as we can stuff in our mouths. So the big decision we're facing at this moment is.... pigs-in-a-blanket or chocolate chip pancakes?

Yes! I got the all clear - at least for now. They pinched and poked and prodded the little pea, from the front, from the sides and upside down. The doctor said he didn't see anything to be concerned about. Or, as the sonogram technician said to me with a shrug, "Women's breasts are lumpy." She also cautioned that, since I'm considered high-risk my doctor will be extra vigilant, and I shouldn't freak out if I have to come back again to have something else checked out.

Although I'm very relieved and grateful, I don't feel much like celebrating. A whipped cream smiley face on my pancake is it for the celebration. It's been an extremely sobering experience. At the Breast Diagnostic Center, there were a half dozen other women, all wearing pink gowns, sitting with me in the interior waiting room. We didn't exchange names, share stories or swap recipes; we barely made eye contact. Still, I can't stop wondering how things turned out for them. They're someone's mother, someone's daughter, someone's sister. I hope they all got good news today.

So, our parks trip is still on, and I'm not going to take a second of it for granted. All doubts I once had about whether we're doing the right thing are gone. As Matt reminds me all the time, "We don't get these days back." Amen, to that. Gotta go; the pancakes are here.

Lots of love,
Karen

From: **Matt Smith**
Subject: **#5 – Rocky Mountain National Park**
Date: **July 21, 2010**

Dear Bob and Sue,

Visiting Rocky Mountain National Park today brought back memories from when our kids were young, and we spent summer vacations in Estes Park. They always enjoyed the town of Estes Park more than the national park. It's hard for rocks, trees and tundra to complete for a child's attention when there are go-carts and a giant slide close by.

I came here as a kid myself. It was my introduction to the national parks. Then, in the 1970's, tourists swarmed Colorado. Developers, it seemed, built as many condominiums as they could get away with – something John Denver could not comprehend – to accommodate the crowds. Against this backdrop, the park became a safe base for people who valued wilderness. Build your golf courses, ski slopes and Olympic Villages along the I-70 corridor, but leave Rocky Mountain National Park unspoiled.

We drove through the park on Trail Ridge Road, entering from the east. The road climbs to the Continental Divide before it loops south to the town of Grand Lake. Workers were re-paving the road, so alternating directions of traffic had to take turns going around them. The drive was slow as we climbed to nearly 12,000 feet. Being so high, the road is above the tree line for a long stretch. One of my favorite family photos is of the kids and me, above the tree line along Trail Ridge Road, with the mountain peaks in the background and clouds below. It looks like we just climbed to a remote summit, instead of driving there in a minivan with a *Fivel Goes West* videotape playing in the back.

Halfway through the park, at the Alpine Visitor Center, we stopped and stamped our passports. At the stamp station, a man wearing a Kansas State t-shirt stood uncomfortably close to me and stared at what I was doing. He watched me stamp my passport, as if I was one of the park's interpretive exhibits. I looked up at him from my passport thinking he wanted to use the stamp or maybe say hello. Why else would he be invading my personal space? Then, he just walked away without grunting a word.

From the visitor center, we drove to Grand Lake. Along the drive, we saw Roosevelt Elk, sometimes in the distance, and sometimes near the road. In a couple of places, they were so close people stopped their cars to take pictures. A man turned off his car in the middle of the road, got out and left his driver's side door open. Oncoming traffic had to drive onto the shoulder of the road to avoid hitting the door. He walked about 30 feet into the grass, and stood with his hands on his hips, looking at the elk while traffic piled up behind him. Bob, by any chance were you in Rocky Mountain National Park today?

We exited the park to the south, and entered the town of Grand Lake where we're staying for two nights. There we could see the widespread damage from the ongoing pine beetle epidemic. It's shocking. Huge areas of pine forest are dying, and it's happening from Mexico to Canada. The park service newsletter says, "There is no effective means of controlling a large beetle outbreak in such a vast area as the park's backcountry, which comprises about 95 percent of the park." The National Park Service's efforts are limited to trying to keep the trees alive near facilities such as visitor centers and campgrounds.

Enough with the beetles; tomorrow we hike.

Your Friend,
Matt

From: **Matt Smith**
Subject: **Rocky Mountain day two**
Date: **July 22, 2010**

Dear Bob and Sue,

Today's main activity was an 11-mile round-trip hike to Lone Pine Lake starting from the East Inlet Trailhead on the west side of Rocky Mountain National Park. A park ranger stood at the entrance of the trail checking hikers on their way in. He was making sure no one was taking a dog on the trail and that everyone had appropriate footwear and clothing. We've seen people wear crazy stuff on hiking trails. (I once saw a woman on Tiger Mountain, a half-mile from the summit, hiking in flip-flops. There was six inches of snow on the ground at the time.) I'm sure he turned a few hikers away today. But not us; he deemed our clothing appropriate and told us to enjoy our hike.

About a mile into the hike, we saw two fox standing on the trail about 30 yards ahead of us. Their coats were thick and fluffy like they just had a bath. We haven't seen many fox in the wild to compare them with, but these two looked very healthy. They didn't seem concerned that we were there, they looked at us and calmly continued on their way.

Another mile or so down the trail, a yellow-bellied marmot ran across our path and then hid among the rocks. I tried to get a good look at him, but he was better at hiding than I was at finding him. I'm 49 years old and as of a month ago I'd never seen a marmot. Since then I've seen four different species: Olympic (Olympic National Park), Hoary (Mount Rainier National Park), groundhog (Michigan, visiting you) and Yellow-Bellied (Rocky Mountain National Park). Four different kinds of marmots in a month! I enthusiastically shared this with Karen, and she said, "No one cares. They're rodents."

No one cares? I care.

As soon as we reached Lone Pine Lake, we stood there looking at it for as long as it took to eat a granola bar, and then turned around to hike back. Karen and I enjoy the hiking part of the hike much more than the sitting and looking part. Karen says she wants us to stop more often and enjoy the scenery on our hikes, but I've tested her on this. Any pause longer than 30 seconds brings a response of, "What are we doing? Are you ready to go?"

The main reason Karen wants to keep moving is she doesn't like to pee on the trail. Many of our hikes are three to four hours long, and often the deciding factor in choosing our hike for the day is which one has a restroom at the end. I don't care where I pee; I'm fine peeing next to the trail. We've made a pact that whenever I stop to pee on a hike Karen's job is to be the lookout. She's supposed to warn me about approaching hikers by calling out, "Whip-poor-will, whip-poor-will." So far, the only thing I've heard from her is heavy exhales. She's jealous that I can pee anywhere. I'm supposed to hold it, in a show of solidarity, until she can go also.

We were lucky that we didn't stay long at Lone Pine Lake. A few minutes after we turned to head for the car, we heard thunder. The sky was nearly cloud free, but we knew afternoon thunderstorms in the Rockies can develop quickly.

We quickened our pace, and each time we heard thunder, we sped up more. A mile from the car, we were surprised to see hikers passing us going in the other direction with no raincoats, backpacks, or umbrellas – no rain gear of any kind. Some even had expensive cameras, out of their cases and hanging around their necks. I could hear Karen behind me say softy, as if talking to the passing hikers, "It's cloudy, it's windy, there's thunder and lightning, you're gonna be drowned rats in about ten minutes."

About a half-mile from the car, we felt small drops and strong wind gusts. Growing up in the Midwest, we're familiar with this; we knew we only had a few minutes before the heavy rain would reach us. The last 200 yards was a dash for the car through a downpour and small hail. We sat in the car, dripping wet, watching it rain and feeling the car rock back and forth from the wind. As strange as it sounds, we miss thunderstorms (Seattle rarely has thunderstorms). It was a perfect end to a perfect hike.

Tomorrow we're driving to Black Canyon of the Gunnison

National Park. I have to confess; I don't know what a Gunnison is.

Your Friend,
Matt

From: **Matt Smith**
Subject: **#6 – Black Canyon of the Gunnison National Park**
Date: **July 24, 2010**

Dear Bob and Sue,

We must look soft. Ranger Betty at the BCoftheG Visitor Center seemed to think so. We told her that we wanted to do the Gunnison Route hike from the rim of the canyon down to the river, but she strongly discouraged us. She listed many reasons why we shouldn't do that hike, including that it's one mile down to the river, but an 1,800-foot vertical drop. It's so steep the park service installed an 80-foot chain, a third of the way down the trail, to assist hikers. Betty tried to convince us that we weren't prepared for the hike by pointing out that we didn't have gloves; we weren't wearing long pants, and we didn't have the recommended gallon of water each. But we insisted on trying anyway. We thought, "It's a short hike, how hard could it be?" Also, when someone tells Karen she can't do something, it only makes her want to do it more.

Hikers are required to get a backcountry permit and listen to an orientation talk before attempting this hike. Betty prepared our permit, then got out her notebook with the orientation script. She began to take us through the orientation: what plants we would encounter (Stinging Nettle and Poison Ivy were my favorites), how to use the chain, etc. About three minutes into the orientation, Karen wandered off to look at postcards. Ranger Betty stopped her presentation; whistled to get Karen's attention and motioned her back. This only deepened Betty's concern about us (mostly Karen).

Once we had Karen with us again, Betty went over the animals we might encounter on the hike. She turned her notebook to a page with a picture of a black bear and a mountain lion. She first pointed to the mountain lion and said, "If you see this one, there's nothing you can do, so I'll tell you about the bear instead." Already, we felt more confident. Betty told us about a black bear that frequents the trail, and what to do if we came across him. After the orientation, we signed the backcountry permit, and were free to do the hike.

On the trail, we quickly learned why ranger Betty tried to discourage us. The beginning of the trail was nearly straight down vertical. We struggled in several places trying not to fall and slide on our butts down the canyon, and we hadn't even gotten to the chain yet. After a quarter of a mile, we called it quits and climbed back up. We had to use our hands to pull ourselves up the trail, grabbing tree trunks and roots. The hike lasted about as long as the orientation.

Part of the deal with backcountry permits is you have to turn them back into the visitor center when you finish the hike, so they know who to go looking for (rescue) at the end of the day. I snuck into the visitor center, hoping to slip the permit to the cashier in the bookstore and leave before Betty saw me. But as if on cue, Betty came around the corner as I reached the counter. I handed her the permit, and silently blamed Karen by tilting my head toward the parking lot. Betty could see her standing out there, fixing her hair in the reflection of our car's window. There was no reason to let Betty think we're both lame.

From the visitor center, we hiked the Flat Oak Loop, then drove the rim road stopping at many of the overlooks. The canyon is very steep and narrow. The views from the overlooks are impressive, but because of the steepness of the canyon, hikes are either flat (along the rim) or nearly vertical (to the river). The rest of our hiking today was along the rim.

It occurred to me as I looked into the canyon that most national parks are defined by what's there: a mountain, a lake, or the wildlife. But, BCoftheG National Park is defined by what's not there; a thin, but incredibly deep, chunk of the high plateau is missing. The Gunnison River has carried it away. Because of the steepness of the canyon, it's a small park in terms of land that can be used for recreation, and there's not much close by. We stayed in the town of Montrose, 13 miles away, which was the closest lodging we could find.

The canyon was a spectacular sight, especially today when it was clear and sunny. But, unless you hike down to the river, it doesn't take long to see the park. We felt we did and saw everything we wanted to in a few hours.

By the way, Karen and I decided the name of the park is too long, so we've shortened it to BCoftheG. Tomorrow we're stopping in Telluride for the night on our way to Mesa Verde National Park.

Your Friend,
Matt

From: **Matt Smith**
Subject: **#7 – Mesa Verde National Park**
Date: **July 26, 2010**

Dear Bob and Sue,

The drive south from Telluride on Highway 145 this morning was spectacular; around every turn, there was a scene of red cliffs and dark green forest against a brilliant blue sky. We even saw a black bear by the side of the road. Ten miles east of Cortez, Colorado, in the southwest corner of the state, we came to the entrance of Mesa Verde National Park.

Today was a bonus day for us. We weren't expecting to get to the park as early as we did. We drove straight to the Far View Visitor Center, and signed up for tours of Balcony House and Cliff Palace; we also got tickets for tomorrow's Mug House and Long House tours. Our timing was perfect. There was just enough time to TCB before driving to Chapin Mesa for the Balcony House tour.

TCB is short for *taking care of business*, not to be confused with *doing your business*, which is Karen's euphemism for going to the bathroom. Specifically, on our parks trip TCB means: 1) Taking our picture in front of the park sign. 2) Getting a copy of the park map and newsletter. 3) Stamping our passports. 4) And, buying four postcards (one for each of our kids and one for us). The only other requirement to make a park visit *official* is to do an activity like a hike or ranger-led tour.

In 1888, two cowboys reported finding cliff dwellings on the mesa, and, from that moment, interest in the area grew quickly. Eventually, concerns about artifacts being removed and the potential for damage to the archeological sites led to the establishment of the park in 1906.

Cliff dwellings are the main attraction at Mesa Verde. There are more than 600 of them in the park, but most are not open to the public. The Pueblo Indians constructed them from about 550 to 1300 AD, although the golden age of cliff dwelling in the area was from 1100 to 1300 AD. Archeologists can tell that the majority of cliff dwellers left abruptly at the end of the 13th century, probably as a result of a 24-year draught and the stress of over-population on the mesa. Most of the dwelling sites are located under eroded areas beneath cliffs; this protected the inhabitants from the weather and from one another.

Balcony House was our first tour today. Our group met in the parking lot for an orientation talk with Jenny, the ranger who was our guide. She explained what we would see, and warned us of the physical requirements of the tour. To enter Balcony House, each member of the group had to climb a 32-foot wooden ladder. It sounded scarier than it was. Later, I asked Jenny if there had ever been accidents on the ladder, or if anyone had ever needed to be rescued from Balcony House. I was surprised when she said that more than once, a person with a heart condition had climbed to the top of the ladder, then after stepping into Balcony House, died of a heart attack.

Jenny led us down a steep set of stairs built into the cliff adjacent to Balcony House. At the bottom was a locked gate; before unlocking it, she turned to the group and said, "This is the last chance for anyone to chicken out gracefully. If you get to the ladder, and don't want to climb it, everyone will have to wait while I walk you back to this gate and let you out." There were no chickens in our group.

Inside the gate, a paved path led us to a spot just beneath Balcony House, and to the foot of the access ladder. It was wide enough for two people to climb side-by-side. I had imagined we would go up one-at-a-time, but the ladder was tall enough for several of us to climb at the same time. Looking up, I was relieved to see only a couple of skinny kids above me – 60-pounders at the most. If they fell, they weren't likely to take me with them. Everyone on our tour made it up the ladder without incident. There were no falls or heart attacks.

Balcony House was a medium sized cliff dwelling; it had 45 rooms and two kivas. Some rooms were a few feet deep and wide, probably built for storage, while others looked large enough for a family to sleep in. A kiva is a room where communal or religious gatherings took place. They are usually round, with a floor several feet below ground level, and have a place to make a fire.

Balcony House faces east; it would have been a cold place to live in the winter, but because of the way they built it into the cliff, it was an easy place to defend. It's a hard place to get into or out of in a hurry. Our exit included crawling through a narrow 12-foot tunnel. A big person would not be able to get through. Another reason for the orientation talk before the tour was to give Jenny a chance to size up the group – literally – and to encourage anyone who might be too big to make it through the tunnel to sit this one out. Once through the tunnel, we climbed another ladder, then we scrambled back up to the mesa using the handholds and toeholds carved into the side of the cliff by the original cliff dwellers.

Usually, we don't like guided tours, but this one we enjoyed; besides, going on a ranger-led tour is the only way to see most of the major cliff dwellings in the park. The park service does this to protect the sites from damage by visitors. Even the smallest wear-and-tear, multiplied thousands of times over the years, can do serious damage to the sites.

After a quick lunch and a visit to the Chapin Mesa Museum, we got in line for our afternoon tour. Cliff Palace is the largest cliff dwelling in North America. It's a magnificent sight from the trail just below the parking lot. From a distance, it looks fake, like an architect's model, until a tour group files in to give it a sense of scale. I can only imagine what those cowboys thought when they first saw these houses.

Cliff Palace was much easier to get into than Balcony House. It only required climbing a couple of short ladders, and there were no tunnels to crawl through. With 150 rooms and 23 kivas, the park service estimates that 100 people lived at Cliff Palace. Karen wanted to stay all afternoon, but the rangers kept us moving. There were more tours scheduled after ours.

With the balance of the afternoon, we hiked the 2.5-mile Petroglyph Point Trail, which goes past one of the largest and best-preserved petroglyph panels in the Southwest.

A petroglyph is a design – often prehistoric - carved into rock; not to be confused with a pictograph, which is a design drawn or painted onto the surface of a rock.

The petroglyphs were clearly visible in the bright afternoon sunlight: spirals, hand prints, zig zags, big horn sheep, human stick figures - one with both arms overhead, another with its right arm up and left arm down. Standing in front of the panel it was exciting to think that another person had stood in that same spot, in the case of these petroglyphs no fewer than 700 years ago, scratching their design into the rock. It's as if the person had just stepped around the corner a few minutes ago.

On the petroglyph trail we met Paula and Gary from Indiana. Later at the Far View Lodge, we ran into them again and had a beer together. They told us about all the parks they've visited; it was an impressive list, even more so considering they drive to them all – they don't like to fly. We told them about our plan to visit all 58 national parks; they were enthusiastic and encouraging. It's fun to connect with other fans of the parks. It gives us the energy to keep going. Bob and Sue, it's not too late for you to join us.

Your Friend,
Matt

From: **Matt Smith**
Subject: **Mesa Verde day two**
Date: **July 27, 2010**

Dear Bob and Sue,

The park newsletter describes the Mug House Tour as a "strenuous two-hour, three-mile round-trip hike that includes... steep drop-offs, switchbacks and scrambling over boulders." That's code for "if you have to rock back-and-forth several times to build up enough momentum to get your ass out of your car, don't sign up for this tour." It's a weed out tactic. The tour is a ranger-led "limited-time-only hike" that the park just started offering to test the level of public interest; this morning we took the 10:00am tour.

There were nine of us on the hike including the two rangers. We were happy to visit this remote cliff dwelling with such a small group. It was sunny and cool, a perfect day for a hike. From the parking lot, we walked about a quarter of a mile along the paved road where we found the trail to the cliff dwelling. We then left the road and walked down a trail through the scrubby, desert-like landscape, watching for rattlesnakes that sometimes sun themselves in the open. After dropping down a few hundred feet in elevation, the path leveled, and then followed the contour of the cliffs until it reached Mug House. When explorers first entered these ruins, they found three mugs hanging in one of the rooms, as if the residents forgot them when they left in a hurry; that's how the site got its name.

The ranger leading the tour had done her homework on Mug House. She and her husband are seasonal rangers, and teachers during the rest of the year. She showed us how archeologists could tell that various sections of the complex were built at different times because of the methods and materials used. She also explained how the cliff dwellers would recycle building materials; when they built a new complex, they got much of their building materials from tearing down older dwellings. This was all thoughtfully prepared and presented in a three-ring binder with plastic page protectors for each exhibit.

Karen and I enjoyed the Mug House tour very much. Being in a small group, and a couple of miles away from the road gave it an intimate and authentic feel. In that setting, we could imagine what it was like for the early explorers of this area when they stumbled across these ruins. Hopefully, the park will continue to offer these backcountry tours.

By noon, we were back at the parking lot where we began; nothing about the hike seemed strenuous like the newsletter suggested. We had just enough time to eat lunch in our rental car and do a self-guided tour of Step House before our 1pm Long House tour.

A tram from the parking lot took our Long House tour group of 40 a few miles along a paved path to a staging area. Long House was the most picturesque dwelling we visited, partly because the lighting was perfect when we were there. The site faces west, and when the afternoon sun hit it, the red stones against the green vegetation made a striking scene. When the late 19th century explorers discovered these ruins, they were jumbles of stones; centuries of silt obscured most of what was beneath. Now, they've been carefully unearthed, but many of the walls remain in mid crumble, their stair step edges suggesting where the complete walls once were. The park service has made modest repairs to some of the structures, but nearly everything visible at the cliff dwellings is from the period of the Pueblo Indians.

Long House was beautiful, but the ranger leading the tour was a bonehead. If he had only pointed and grunted, the tour would have been more enjoyable and educational; a huge difference from the tour this morning.

Most rangers we encounter in the parks are dedicated, enthusiastic and do a great job on the tours. This guy must have slipped through the screening process. At the beginning of the tour, he chose a 12-year old girl from the group, and played "let's pretend you're an Indian girl and you're getting ready for your wedding." (The Pueblo Indians married young 700 years ago.) She had to choose a boy from the group to be her husband, which was awkward and kind of creepy. The rest of the tour involved asking the two of them questions like "what food would you serve at your wedding?" while the rest of us stood around listening to them guess wrong answers. The only thing I hate more than audience participation is guessing games. If the ranger wants us to know that the Pueblo Indians ate beans, corn and squash, then JUST TELL US! The tour was painful and inappropriate, but the site was beautiful. They should make this a silent tour.

During one of the guessing sessions, I instinctively stood up; I had to get away. Karen looked up and whispered, "Where are you going?"

"Back to the car, I wasn't invited to the wedding." She grabbed my leg and said, "You're not going anywhere." She was right. There was no way out. We were a few miles from the parking lot, and the tram would not be back for another 45 minutes. I just had to tough it out.

After the Long House tour, we drove back to Far View Lodge. Mesa Verde is a beautiful park to drive through. It's a plateau ranging from 7,000 to 8,000 feet in elevation. Juniper and pinyon trees normally cover much of the park, but nine sizable forest fires over the last 100 years have wiped many of them out. A ranger told us that the re-growth cycle for juniper trees after a fire is about 250 years. At 400 years old, the juniper and pinyon tree forest gets so thick it's susceptible to a major fire – usually caused by lightning – and so the cycle continues. Two fires in the year 2000 burned more than 28,000 acres in the park. We could still see the impact of those fires today as we drove through the park.

As we were driving to the lodge, a heavy thunderstorm blew in. It was perfect timing. We'd finished our day of tours, and welcomed the cool break. We ate at the lodge restaurant for the second night in a row. It was fantastic: Indian rugs on the walls, professional wait staff and interesting menu items. I ordered the Poblano Rellenos that Karen had last night. We'll have to make it for you next time we're together.

Your Friend,

Matt

From: **Karen Smith**
Subject: **#8 – Great Sand Dunes National Park**
Date: **July 28, 2010**

Dear Bob and Sue,

Walking from the parking lot onto the sand at Great Sand Dunes National Park was like stepping onto a beach, minus the ocean. There were people in swimming suits lounging in beach chairs, toddlers running around in diapers, kids building sand castles and throwing Frisbees. It didn't seem like we were in south central Colorado.

In the spring, Medano Creek runs along the eastern edge of the dune field, between the parking area and the dunes. In May, visitors can experience surge flows. Sand creates small dams upstream in the creek, and when the water breaks through, waves up to 12″ high, flow downstream. In wet years, with high runoff, people float, surf and skimboard down the waves. The creek area is crowded during May and June weekends, causing lines of traffic and overflowing parking lots. The creek bed was dry today, but the beachgoers didn't seem to mind.

The Great Sand Dunes are the tallest dunes in North America, rising in front of the Sangre de Cristo Mountains, they're a dramatic sight. We stopped at the visitor center first, and then set off to hike to the top of one of the dunes, about a 700-foot rise, *in the middle of the afternoon.* This was a serious lapse of common sense. In the summer, you should avoid the dunes during the afternoon. The ranger at the visitor center told us this, but we ignored her advice. The air temperature is brutally hot, and, of course, the sand gets even hotter. The surface temperature on the dunes can reach 140 degrees. We were also starting at a high elevation, 8,200 feet, which meant we were breathing heavily just walking through the parking lot.

Minutes into the hike, the wind started blowing sand into our eyes and faces; it stung our bare arms and legs. It was all very painful. We had to close our eyes to keep the sand from blinding us. The sand stuck to our sweat, and I was sweating pretty much everywhere. Walking was slow and difficult. With every step, our feet would sink and our shoes filled with sand. We tied our shoelaces as tight as possible, but the sand found a way in regardless. Eventually, there was no room in our shoes for our feet and toes to move. Every few minutes, we had to take off our shoes, balance on one foot, - because it was too hot to place the other foot on the sand – and dump out the sand. There was no way to keep the sand out.

Occasionally, I would pry open my eyes to see where I was going. I could barely make out the shape of Matt's body ahead in the sandstorm. I did my best to keep up with him, but I was miserable. The only thing that kept me going was envisioning how much younger I was going to look with the top layer of my skin sandblasted off.

The sand dunes kicked our asses. We didn't make it to the top. On our way back to the car, we saw people having way more fun than we were. They were sand boarding and sledding on the dunes, dragging everything from snowboards to cookie sheets with them. Some were also dragging their dogs. They must not have seen the signs warning that dogs shouldn't be on the dunes after 11am in the summer because their paws will burn on the hot sand. Dogs can't tell their owners when their paws are on fire.

We learned a few hard lessons today. Our negative experience wasn't because it's a bad park; it was due to our poor planning. We should have allowed ourselves another day to spend in this park. The mountains and forests surrounding the dunes are beautiful, and there are some great hikes we missed. And of course, we should have hiked the dunes in the early morning or evening.

I wish we had time to go back tomorrow morning and give it another try, but we're heading to Lawrence, Kansas to be with Matthew on his birthday. Along the way, we're planning to visit a couple of more national park units: Bent's Old Fort National Historic Site and Fort Larned National Historic Site. Then, if we have time during our stay in Kansas City, we'll go to Independence, Missouri to visit the Harry S. Truman National

Historic Site. Even though these sites aren't named *national parks,* we still enjoy visiting them when we're in the area, so long as they have a stamp for our passports.

Your friend,
Karen

From: **Matt Smith**
Subject: **Travel day - to Holbrook, Arizona**
Date: **August 10, 2010**

Dear Bob and Sue,

Bob, you will appreciate this (because you're cheap like me). At 5:54am this morning, we took the No. 218 bus from the Issaquah Park and Ride to the International District in Seattle, where we caught the light rail to SeaTac airport. The total cost for the two of us was $6.50. That's one-tenth the cost of a taxi and way cheaper than parking at the airport.

We flew to Las Vegas where we picked up a rental car for the week. Our plan is to drive to Petrified Forest National Park, then to Grand Canyon National Park and then back to Las Vegas to celebrate Karen's 50th birthday this weekend.

Karen's name for the week is "Fitty." She doesn't like it when I call her fitty, she said, "No one over the age of 40 knows what fitty means. It's confusing. People will think you're calling me that because I'm so physically fit." I told her that I was willing to take that chance.

On our way east to Holbrook, Arizona, we stopped in Flagstaff. Downtown Flag (Flag is what the locals call Flagstaff) has several decent outdoor gear stores. I found a backpack that I'd been looking for, and as I took it to the cashier Karen reminded me that she had officially banned me from buying any more backpacks. (I just bought one last month, and have a couple of others.) I explained to her, "I can't have just one backpack. That would be lame. They're all different sizes and made for different activities." She said, "You mean like purses? Why didn't you say that in the first place? Now I get it. A backpack is your man-purse."

I started to tell her that she didn't know what she was talking about, *and* that she doesn't have authority to ban me from doing anything, but she was already gone. She was looking through the backpacks to see if there was one that matched my hiking boots.

Earlier, when we were exploring the town, we'd stopped in the Lumberyard Brewery for a beer. Since we didn't know what kind of restaurants we'd find in Holbrook, we headed back to the brewery and had an early dinner. Flagstaff has everything we like in a city: it's a college town, high in elevation, with good breweries and endless outdoor recreation opportunities. We could live here.

When we finished dinner we drove to Holbrook and checked into the Travel Lodge. It's an older motel that looked sketchy on the outside, but the room was nice and clean (and inexpensive). The person who checked us in was extremely helpful; he gave me a map of the area and showed me quickest way to get to Petrified Forest National Park. If we're ever in Holbrook again, we would stay here. Karen went to bed at 8:30pm, (7:30pm pacific time). That's a new record.

Your Friend,
Matt

From: **Matt Smith**
Subject: **#9 – Petrified Forest National Park**
Date: **August 11, 2010**

Dear Bob and Sue,

When we got to the Petrified Forest National Park Visitor Center, I noticed that their passport stamp was misshapen and hard to read. I was hoping all the stamps would be the same size, style and quality so they would look orderly when I frame them together after our parks trip is complete. That's just OC, right, no D? I said to Karen, "You didn't even notice that the stamp looked different from the others. That's the opposite of OC. There should be a name for *that.*" She said, "There is. It's called *normal.*"

I don't think so.

From the visitor center, we hiked about a half-mile to the Painted Desert Inn. It was an interesting hike because of the incredible views of the surrounding Painted Desert. The colors were incredible. The inn is no longer structurally stable enough to allow overnight guests. Now, it's a national historic landmark, and functions only as a museum and bookstore. You can look in the windows of the original guest rooms; they are small and primitive.

There's a fantastic petroglyph of a mountain lion displayed inside the inn. The ranger in the gift store said that during construction of the inn workers building the road flipped over the rock and found the petroglyph on the back. It makes me wonder how many great petroglyphs are out in the desert that will never be found.

Ten miles to the south of the inn is Blue Mesa. It gets its name from the bluish bentonite clay on the mesa. We hiked the one-mile Blue Mesa Loop; there we saw lots of petrified wood, but mostly in small pieces. Karen thinks the park should be renamed Petrified Pieces National Park because there is no forest; all the petrified wood is laying on the ground in pieces. I'm not bothered by this fact. Now who has the OC?

The Puerco Pueblo ruins, just north of Blue Mesa, are the remains of a 100-room pueblo (occupied between 1,200 and 700 years ago). Close to the ruins, we saw several petroglyphs near the paved trail. My favorite was one of a large bird with a baby in its beak. Not a baby bird, a baby human. No one knows why the bird has a baby in its beak. Karen is sure the bird was bringing a baby to a family, rather than carrying a baby away. I'm not so sure.

We drove to the Rainbow Forest Museum in the southwest corner of the park. Behind the museum, we walked through an area with giant logs of petrified wood. The name of the trail is, surprisingly, the Giant Logs Trail. It takes visitors through one of the best-preserved areas of petrified wood in the park. The size and number of logs is amazing. Karen was more impressed with these specimens but still wouldn't call it a forest. This area once had many more times the number of large, petrified logs than it has today. Before the area became a national park, prospectors hauled away train carloads of petrified wood. Much of it was ground up for use as industrial abrasive. That's a real shame; I wish I could have seen this area before that happened.

We had to wrap up our visit early; we had a long drive to get to the Grand Canyon where we are spending the night.

Your Friend,
Matt

From: **Matt Smith**
Subject: **#10 – Grand Canyon National Park**
Date: **August 12, 2010**

Dear Bob and Sue,

Yesterday on the way to the Grand Canyon, we stopped at the Cameron Trading Post because we'd heard it had a huge selection of Navajo rugs. Their rugs were fantastic but out of our price range. Along the road from the trading post to the park's east entrance there were roadside stands selling Navajo art and crafts. We stopped at a couple but didn't buy anything. It was so windy that the pottery on the tables wobbled constantly. I kept imagining having to buy an entire table of vases because we were standing there when a strong gust came by.

Our first stop inside the park was the Desert View lookout. The sun was setting, and the light was perfect. It was the golden hour. The views were amazing. It's the Grand Canyon; what can I say? Any description would be inadequate, so I'm not even going to try. It's a must see wonder.

We drove along the canyon rim stopping at a couple of overlooks, then to the Grand Canyon Village where we ate dinner in the El Tovar Hotel bar. We had tried to get a reservation to stay overnight in the hotel, but it sold out months ago, and we were too late in making our plans. Instead, we stayed at the Best Western just outside the park.

The Grand Canyon is an incredible sight to see, but this time of year the park is overcrowded. Before we finish our national parks tour, we plan on visiting the north rim of the canyon and hiking to the bottom and back. This morning we just wanted to do a half-day hike. We got to parking lot E in the Village at 7:45am and were hiking down Bright Angel Trail before 8:00am. There wasn't a cloud in the sky.

You want to get on the Bright Angel Trail early. Tour companies use this trail to take people down to the river on mules. They don't slow you down so much as they leave presents along the trail. Early in the day there's less mule shit to step around.

The hike to the canyon floor on Bright Angel Trail is about seven miles. Today, we were hoping to hike four miles down, but when we got to the three-mile rest stop at 9am it was getting so hot we decided it was a good time to turn around. Since the hardest part of the hike is going uphill, we wanted to make sure we'd have enough energy to make it back. From our rest stop, we had 2,000 vertical feet to climb to get back to the top of the trail. We rested for 20 minutes, and then started our return.

There's an attitude change that happens when you switch directions on a steep hike. On the downhill side, everything is right with the world. Steps are effortless, and views are spectacular; you greet every passing hiker with a smile and, "Good morning!" Karen might even convince me to hold her hand and laugh now and then. But the way up is a trudge. Every other breath is a gasp; your aching legs feel thick and heavy, and all you want to say to passing hikers is, "No, it's not a good morning; stop smiling, and get out of my way before I pass out."

Hiking up the canyon, there's no bailing out; you have to make it to the top to get out. Time slows, and you lose perspective on how much farther you have to go. But, we've found a reliable method of determining how close we are to the parking lot by looking at passing hikers. The first sign that we were getting close to the top was when we passed a husband and wife with two small children. The kids looked to be about four and six years old. The four-year old was making himself dizzy by twirling in circles with his arms straight out, the father trying to keep him from spinning off the side of the canyon, while the mother tried to console the six-year old who was sitting hunched over, arms crossed and with tears running down his cheeks. That's as good of a one-mile marker as there is on a trail like this.

A short distance past the happy family, we stopped to take a drink of water. We were both sweating heavily and glad we'd brought plenty of water. I looked at Karen and said, "Nice red underwear." There was no response, just a confused look on her face. "Your white shorts are completely see-through." Karen had been sweating so much that her hiking shorts were transparent.

That may explain why no one passed us on the way up the trail.

I dug an extra t-shirt out of my backpack; Karen tied it around her waist, and we continued our death march to the top. Finally, I looked up to see a woman coming toward us wearing shiny gold flip-flops, designer jeans that were tight enough to be body paint and a black t-shirt with the words "Wine Tester" spelled out in bright red sequins. That was a sure sign we were less than a quarter of a mile from the car.

We reached the top of the canyon well before noon. As soon as we were off the trail and on flat ground, we regretted not having gone farther down the trail; we had plenty of energy left. The park service warns people not to attempt hiking down to the bottom of the canyon and back up in the same day, but everyone needs to know their own fitness level and adjust that advice accordingly. Families with small children and wine testers certainly aren't going to make it, but a down-and-back hike in one day is doable for people in good shape. Still, I wouldn't try it in August (especially hiking with someone who's about to turn 50). Tomorrow we're driving to Las Vegas to celebrate Karen's birthday, and then next week we're off to Alaska.

Your Friend,
Matt

From: **Matt Smith**
Subject: **#11 – Glacier Bay National Park**
Date: **August 18, 2010**

Dear Bob and Sue,

Alaska is big. Things here are on a different scale than in the lower 48 states; Glacier Bay National Park is about the size of Connecticut, yet there are four national parks in Alaska even bigger.

It was easier than we thought it would be to get here. The flight from Seattle to Juneau was two and a half hours, and from Juneau to Gustavus the flight was 14 minutes. Four minutes into our flight to Gustavus the pilot asked the flight attendants to prepare for landing; I was timing it. By late afternoon, we were sitting on the deck of Glacier Bay Lodge, having a beer and looking out over Bartlett Cove. I asked our waitress if Bartlett Cove had been named after President Bartlett. Karen interrupted by saying, "Ignore him. He's an idiot." Well, this idiot got us to Alaska. Seeing Alaska has been at the top of Karen's wish list ever since we moved to Seattle, and now we're here.

The town of Gustavus has 346 permanent residents and an airport large enough to land a 737. The federal government subsidizes the airport as part of its Essential Air Service program. There's no other way a town this remote could support such a large airport.

At the airport, we boarded a Glacier Bay Lodge school bus along with the other guests. Our driver gave us the nickel tour from the airport to the lodge. He stopped briefly in town, which the locals call the "intersection" where there's a gas station, pizza place and art gallery. A couple of miles past the intersection, we came to the Glacier Bay National Park boundary. It's one of the few sections of the road from the airport to the lodge that's not heavily treed. It's called the moose flats because moose often stop there to feed.

"There are always moose here," the driver said. "When I drove past here ten minutes ago, there was a moose standing right by the park sign." Fifteen faces pressed against the windows, and the bus tilted a little to the sign side of the road. Everyone who comes to Alaska wants to see a moose. There was no moose.

We ate dinner at the lodge, and afterwards walked down the pier to the docks along the water. It had been a cloudy day, but while we were walking along the docks the sun came out. It was refreshing to feel the sun on our faces. There's a park sign at the end of the pier that welcomes visitors who arrive by boat; we asked a passerby to take our picture in front of it. The sun was in perfect position.

We're excited to be in Alaska, finally. Tomorrow we are taking an all-day boat tour of Glacier Bay.

Your Friend,
Matt

From: **Matt Smith**
Subject: **Glacier Bay day two**
Date: **August 19, 2010**

Dear Bob and Sue,

Today was our boat tour of Glacier Bay National Park. It was raining and in the mid 50's; August here feels like October in Seattle. Ten minutes into our tour the captain spotted a sea otter. He slowed down while the passengers crowded to the otter side of the boat. There was chatter in many different languages, and everyone took pictures or videos. This was our first wildlife sighting of the day. As the boat pulled away, I wondered if we would see more otters. Was that the lone otter or were there others? In the next 30 minutes we saw hundreds of otters. If anyone had fallen overboard they could have walked across otter stomachs all the way to shore without getting wet.

Otterfest was only the beginning of our wildlife sightings. Our next stop was just off South Marble Island where sea lions rested on rocks trying to dry out. The biggest ones got the highest spots where they could dry out the quickest. There was a clear pecking order, and everyone knew his place. The slightest nudge from a smaller sea lion below brought a loud growl and showing of teeth from the one above. The youngest ones were in the water, each looking for a place to climb ashore without getting a chunk taken out of his backside.

At a tidal inlet just past Tlingit Point, we spotted two pair of grizzly bears on the beach. I always thought grizzlies weren't afraid of anything, but after watching these bears it's clear they're afraid of one another. One pair was fishing in a stream close to the shore, until the second pair ran them off.

Some wildlife experts are snobbish about the names people use for bears. They say the correct name for a grizzly bear is brown bear. Although, a black bear can be brown, which doesn't make it a brown bear, it's just a black bear that's brown. Karen likes cinnamon bears, because she likes the sound of the name. Cinnamon bears are usually black bears, but brown bears can also be cinnamon – in color. The way to tell them apart is that grizzlies have a distinct shoulder hump and smaller ears than black bears. I don't care what others think; I'm going to keep calling brown bears grizzlies from now on.

The wildlife sightings continued. We spotted humpback whales off Willoughby Island. On Gloomy Knob, we saw mountain goats high on the cliffs through our binoculars. Across the bay, on Gilbert Peninsula, a whale carcass had washed onto the beach. Our national park ranger guide, Jane, explained that animals had been taking turns feeding off the carcass for several months. There were no animals feeding on the carcass when we went by. I'm guessing an animal needs to get pretty hungry before it starts in on a whale carcass that's been dead for three months.

We saw many bald eagles, and countless other birds. Jane explained in detail the fascinating nesting and feeding habits of the birds we saw. I don't remember any of their names. We were standing close to Jane when she said, "Now, if you are keeping a life list of birds be sure to write down the 'such and such' bird that we just saw." A life list of birds? Who keeps a life list of birds? I turned to Karen, and in a panicked voice said, "Karen, do you have my life list of birds? I can't find it. You had it last, remember?" Karen caught Jane's eye, tilted her head toward me and said, "Ignore him. He's an idiot."

A massive cruise ship was making its way out of Johns Hopkins Inlet as we headed toward the entrance. Johns Hopkins Glacier dumps into the bay at the end of this inlet. Two hundred years ago, Glacier Bay didn't exist. A glacier extended all the way to where the town of Gustavus is today. Since then, the glacier has receded more than 60 miles. Johns Hopkins Glacier is a remnant of the original glacier that had covered the area that is now the bay.

At the head of the inlet, the captain eased the boat to within a half-mile of the glacier. The passengers again crowded to one side of the boat. I was four or five passengers back from the boat's railing and was not able to get a good view. The captain slowly spun the boat 360 degrees, so everyone got a turn at being in front. He obviously had done this before.

Up to this point in the tour, there was a constant din of conversation from the passengers, but as we stood together looking at the glacier, everyone was silent. Every couple of minutes, thunder would roll across the water and over our boat. House size chunks of ice were breaking off the glacier and falling into the bay. The water around us was turquoise. Through my binoculars, I could see a torrent pouring out from beneath the 170-foot tall wall of ice. Even on cool summer days, a tremendous amount of ice melts. There was a raft of brown ice chunks floating in front of the glacier. The ice looked dirty. Jane explained over the public address system why we had to keep our distance from the glacier; those spots on the ice weren't dirt, they were *seals*. They use this area as a breeding ground, and boats the size of ours must stay at least a quarter of a mile away.

I fell asleep on the boat ride back from the glacier. I had just eaten lunch; it was raining, and the sound of the boat's engines made me sleepy. The last words I remember hearing before falling asleep were Jane's over the public address speaker saying, "If you fall asleep now it will be the most expensive nap you'll ever take." The tour cost $185 per person. I had a good nap, but dreamt I lost my life list of birds.

Your Friend,
Matt

From: **Karen Smith**
Subject: **Glacier Bay day three**
Date: **August 20, 2010**

Dear Bob and Sue,

In the park, there are bear warnings everywhere. Matt and I were nervous about hiking by ourselves, so we did something we never do. We signed up for the daily ranger-led group hike. Matt worries he will get stuck with slow-walkers or loud talkers, but luckily today we were the only ones who showed up. We had a private tour of the Bartlett River Trail with ranger Kevin Richards. The park service closed the trail a few days ago because a brown bear charged a hiker along the river. Kevin had bear spray with him, but I wondered if park rangers pledge an oath promising to defend and protect park visitors, or if a bear charges us, it's every man for himself. Matt always tells people that he doesn't have to run faster than the bear, just faster than me. In case of a bear encounter, ranger Kevin might be my only hope.

The Bartlett River Trail meanders several miles along an intertidal lagoon. Then it cuts through the forest before ending at the Bartlett River estuary. We spent three hours with Kevin, the first two hiking the river trail and the last hour in the lodge talking about our parks trip. From the stories he told us, it sounded like he's been to most of the 58 national parks. He wrote out hiking suggestions for many of the parks in California and Utah. Kevin's enthusiasm and passion for the parks made us even more excited to visit them all.

After lunch, we rented well-used bikes at the lodge and rode eight miles into Gustavus to sightsee and buy beer. We figured if we bought a six-pack of beer at the market it would be cheaper than buying $5 beers at the lodge bar. The ride was flat and easy, except for a small incline near the lodge. A worker at the lodge told us that moose have chased bikers along the park road. I was a little nervous about whether I could out pedal a moose if we ran into one. Visitors to Alaska are always worried about bear encounters, but moose injure more people each year than bears. They tell you to watch for signs that the moose is upset. If its ears are laid back and hackles are up, it's likely to charge. Neither Matt nor I know what a hackle is; we just hope that if a moose raises his we'll be able to spot it.

When we got to the market - the only one in town - we searched up and down the aisles for beer. I could see Matt walk slowly at first and then speed up as reality set in. He circled the store twice, but there was no beer. I finally asked the 16-year old stocking the shelves if the store sold beer. He loudly told us the only place that sells beer is the town liquor store, open from 4-7pm each day. It was 2:30pm. Everyone in the store was looking at us. We felt stupid not buying anything, so $12 later we had a bag of blue corn chips, a cherry Chapstick, a rubber bouncy ball, a moose shaped Christmas ornament, a Snickers for Matt and a purple Pixie Stix for me.

Since we had 90 minutes to kill before the liquor store opened, we sat on the porch swing in front of the market, eating our candy and swinging back and forth like a couple of 80-year olds. There was a scale next to the swing for weighing nails; Matt weighed all the things we had bought in the store, and then everything in his pockets. It started to rain. I felt like we were in an episode of Northern Exposure.

We entertained ourselves by watching the locals come and go. An elderly native woman walked past us and into the store. She then came back out empty-handed and sat on the porch with us. When Matt went over to our bikes to tighten my wobbly handlebars she sidled up to me. She whispered, "Guess what? I saw a white moose while walking to the store today. I've never seen a white moose before. I came to buy a Pepsi, but I don't have enough money."

I gave her the three dollars I had in my pocket, mostly because it was the right thing to do, but partly because I don't ever want to be on the bad side of a native woman who's seen a white moose, be it real or imagined. I figured I was buying myself curse insurance for the price of a Pepsi. I hope the policy covers spouses, because her wandering eye kept looking over at Matt.

As the rain let up, we rode our bikes down to the water's edge by the public docks and walked along the beach. Gulls were circling and landing by something thrashing in the water. We pulled out our binoculars and could see it was a sea lion wrestling a halibut. The halibut was *huge,* but the size and strength of the sea lion was even more impressive. He was clearly winning. Sea lions may look lazy and awkward when they're sunning themselves on the rocks, but in the water, chomping on a halibut with his mouth open and teeth flashing, this one looked fierce.

At 4:01pm we peddled up to the liquor store. We bought a six-pack paying double what we would at home, and stuffed the bottles in our backpacks. Riding back to Glacier Bay Lodge, we again carefully looked for moose by the moose flats. We didn't see any there, but a mile farther down the road a moose suddenly stepped out from the woods. Not a white moose, but still he was spectacular: huge, dark and shiny, with a dumb look on his face. We stopped about 50 yards away and looked at the moose. The moose looked back. He was very sweet, but there was no way we were going to try to ride past him. After a few minutes, cars came down the road, and the moose disappeared back into the woods.

After dinner, we walked the forest loop by the lodge. At the end of the loop, when the sun was almost down, we saw a moose and her baby eating by the side of the road. The mother moose was wearing a bright orange tracking collar that had "Number 2" written on it. Even though there were people watching them and taking pictures, both mother and baby seemed calm. Their ears weren't back, and there was no sign of hackles.

Hiking, biking, beer and moose. What a great day. Oh yeah, and about that beer that we rode 16 miles to get so we could save some money. Between the bike rentals and the cost of the six-pack, each beer ended up costing about $8.

Your Friend,
Karen

From: **Matt Smith**
Subject: **Out of Gustavus**
Date: **August 21, 2010**

Dear Bob & Sue,

We had all day to kill in Gustavus, as our plane to Anchorage didn't leave until late afternoon. Karen and I rented bikes again and then rode to the only restaurant in town. We sat outside and ordered a large pizza. Once the pizza came, the owner's dog, Shorty, was our friend. Shorty never begged, but I fed him some sausage pizza anyway. Just about the best thing that can happen to a dog is for a stranger to give it sausage pizza. I felt proud of myself for making Shorty's day, until the woman at the next table coaxed him over and started petting him. When the waitress came around, the woman asked if it would be OK to give him a scrap of pizza crust. The waitress said, "Oh no, he's not supposed to have pizza. He'll get sick."

"Check please!"

Our flight out of Gustavus was an hour and a half late departing. It was the last Alaska Airlines flight out of Gustavus for the season. Every "guys week in Alaska" fishing group had booked the same flight. Each group had boxes of frozen fish they were taking with them on the flight. The TSA crew struggled with processing the mass of cargo and passengers.

The flight crew used the extra time to take pictures of themselves in and around the plane. All the passengers watched from the boarding area. We could see the crew through the wall of glass separating us from the tarmac. Each time they posed, we cheered mockingly. The crowd was getting restless; the flight was already an hour past its scheduled departure time. One flight attendant would pose sitting in the cockpit, with her head stuck out the open window, then with much wriggling about another flight attendant would appear a few minutes later, waving to the camera.

Down on the tarmac, they took turns having their picture taken while sitting inside the cowl of the 737's engine. Three of the crew sat inside the engine while a different crewmember took their picture. I'm not sure the 737 was designed to hold the weight of three people sitting *in* the engine.

When it was time to take off, I no longer worried about the engines; I was just glad to be going.

Your Friend,
Matt

From: **Matt Smith**
Subject: **Travel day - to Copper Center, Alaska**
Date: **August 22, 2010**

Dear Bob & Sue,

This morning Karen and I almost hit a moose while driving
to a grocery store. It scared the bejesus out of me. We turned a
corner, and he was right there, standing by the side of the road
eating leaves that were sticking through a chain-link fence. I
drove slowly past trying not to spook him into running in front
of our car. He (or she) is one of a few hundred moose who roam
Anchorage in the summer; in the winter, the number increases to
one thousand or more. A couple of hundred city moose die each
year: cars hit them, they starve, or they die of illness. The State of
Alaska says that a live moose belongs to the state, and a dead
moose belongs to whoever owns the property it's on. In
Anchorage, if a moose dies on your property it's your problem,
and since they can weigh more than a thousand pounds, it's a
pretty big problem. It can cost close to $300 to have a moose
retrieval company drag a moose carcass off your lawn. That's if
you know it's there. Sometimes people don't realize they have
this problem until the spring thaw reveals the gift nature has left
them.

Being Sunday, there wasn't much traffic on our three-hour
drive from Anchorage to Copper Center, a small town just
outside Wrangell-St. Elias National Park. Copper Center has a
population of about 450, including the nearby native village of
Kluti Kaah. We're staying in Copper Center because it has a new
lodge, and it's close to the park and the new Wrangell–St. Elias
Visitor Center. (FYI – Wrangell-St. Elias National Park is
nowhere near Wrangell, Alaska.)

*The Copper River, which flows past Copper Center, is famous in the
lower 48 states for its salmon. One of the most rugged rivers in Alaska, it
begins at Copper Glacier deep inside the park on the northern edge of the
Wrangell Mountains. The river defines the western border of the park as it*

flows south toward the Gulf of Alaska. Every May, around the 15th, the first salmon of the season return to the river: Copper River Kings and Sockeyes. In some years, commercial fishermen catch more than a million Copper River salmon. (The commercial fishing happens south of the park boundaries near the mouth of the river.)

By the time we reached Glenallen, the small town just before Copper Center, it was just past noon - lunchtime and beer time. We tried to buy beer in Anchorage this morning, but in Alaska, it's illegal to sell beer before noon on Sunday. We headed straight for the grocery store, but after searching in vain for beer, we were told by the store clerk that the town was dry. Yikes! My research assistant (Karen) should have learned this before we got to the Edge of Nowhere, Alaska. We contemplated eating pizza at the restaurant across the street, or Thai food from the trailer at the end of the block, but decided on driving to our hotel, the Princess Lodge, in hopes they were serving lunch, and that Copper Center was not dry like Glenallen.

Princess Cruise Line owns the lodge. They bus their cruise passengers to the hotel and set them up with activities like river rafting, fishing and flightseeing.

We checked in and took our luggage to our room. It smelled like old-lady perfume. I thought about asking for another room, but there were two busloads of new guests arriving, and I was too hungry to stand in a long line. Karen gets concerned when I mention that our hotel room smells. She knows what usually follows: she has to get off the bed, put her shoes back on, gather her things that are thrown around the room, drag them all the way back to the front desk, stand there embarrassed while I tell the manager our room smells, drag her stuff to another room and wait while I decide if the new room smells. I spared Karen this time. If the crowd in the lobby was any indication of their typical clientele, all the rooms probably smelled like old-lady perfume anyway. I opened a window and we went looking for food.

After we ate lunch at our hotel, and took care of business at the visitor center, we drove 20 miles north to the historic

Gakona Lodge to check it out. Karen had read an article about the lodge, and was interested in seeing it. (Her real interest was their Trading Post, even though she had nothing to trade.) Built in 1904, it's one of the few remaining roadhouses left in Alaska. The original roadhouse had living quarters, a kitchen/dining room, a few private rooms, an upstairs dormitory and a store. A telegraph station stood nearby. In the early 20th century, there were roadhouses located every 20 miles or so, the distance a person could reasonably travel in a day without an automobile. Only a couple of the original roadhouses in Alaska are still around today; most of the others have burned down.

Inside the lodge's Trappers Den Tavern, we met Greg and Val the owners; he was bartending and she was cooking dinner. Everyone in the bar was friendly. We heard some interesting viewpoints from the locals about living in Alaska. A guy at the bar told us that residents resented the federal government setting the rules about what can and can't be done within the park boundaries. His point was that locals were using the land long before it was made a national park and they should be allowed to continue to use it as before. I told him that I had a different perspective; I felt the national park land belongs to us all, and the park service is stewarding it for us and for future generations. He said he had met the park superintendent recently on a float trip, and she echoed my opinion. Despite his complaints, I could tell he was appreciative of the work the park service had done to preserve the land and create access for people like himself who love to spend time there.

He told me how he enjoyed fishing on the Copper River. He went on to describe how he feels when he's in the park, going to Copper Lake in the winter, and how pristine the area is, especially covered in snow. As he started to tell me what it's like to see Copper Glacier, and to know it's the birth of a river, his voice trailed off. He couldn't continue. Here a man, hardened by 30 years of living in Alaska, choking up about his experience in the wilderness. He said he and his buddies were going back to Copper Lake in March, and invited me to go with them.

We drove back to the Princess Lodge and had dinner. Afterward, Karen and I sat by the two-story window in the great room, watching Mt. Drum slowly change colors as the sun went down. It was a great place to sit quietly and enjoy the sunset. Two women plopped down next to us, neither of them looked at the incredible scene out the window. They talked loudly about the weather in St. Louis, who was hosting bridge tonight back home, and how the Cardinals were doing this year. I've never understood why people spend so much time, energy and money to travel to a distant place, and then wish they were home. Just stay home, it's cheaper.

When our loud neighbors pulled out pictures of their grandchildren and starting talking baby talk, I stood up, turned to Karen and said, "That's it." We were tired anyway and needed to get a good night's sleep, so we walked back to our room and called it a day. Tomorrow we're driving into the park, just the two of us.

Your Friend,
Matt

From: **Karen Smith**
Subject: **#12 – Wrangell-St. Elias National Park**
Date: **August 23, 2010**

Dear Bob & Sue,

On our way out of the hotel this morning, we were surprised to see that all the other guests had set their luggage in the hallway right outside their door. Apparently, a cruise company employee comes by, picks up the luggage from the guest's door, and transports it to the next hotel room (or cruise cabin) where they will be staying that night. Having someone else cart your luggage all over Alaska clearly gives you permission to bring multiple big-ass suitcases and over pack them. I'm a little bit jealous. For as long as I've known Matt, he's had a strict "You pack it, you carry it" rule. No exceptions. If I ever left my luggage outside our door expecting him to transport it to our next destination, I'd be going commando for the rest of the trip.

Today we visited Wrangell–St. Elias National Park and Preserve. It's the big kahuna of the national parks; with more than 13 million acres, it's the size of six Yellowstones.

Four major mountain ranges meet in the park, including nine of the 16 highest peaks in the United States. The west boundary of the park runs along the Canadian border, on the other side is Canada's Kluane National Park. Just one of Wrangell-St. Elias' glaciers, the Malaspina Glacier, is larger than the state of Rhode Island and 2,000 feet thick in places. Because of the park's sheer size, vast mountain ranges and limited road access, it's impossible to see the entire park and grasp its enormity unless you fly over it.

There are only two roads into Wrangell-St. Elias, and both of these dusty dead-end roads are unpaved and occasionally impassable. Before starting out on either of them, it's advised to have: a high clearance vehicle, a full tank of gas, a tire jack and full-size spare tire, flares, automobile insurance, a jumbo-size bag of animal crackers and enough water to last for a couple of days. Nabesna Road, on the north side of the park, is a 42-mile stretch

73

of road originally built by the Alaska Road Commission in 1933 to connect the Nabesna Mine to the port in Valdez. There are no services or communities along the road, mainly it's an access into the park for people who want to camp, hike, fish and hunt.

Hunting is not allowed in most national parks, but there are exceptions in some of the Alaska parks, including Wrangell-St. Elias. When the park was created in 1980, by the passage of the Alaska National Interest Lands Conservation Act (ANILCA), compromises were made. Local residents are allowed to subsistence hunt and gather food to feed their families inside the national park. The national *preserve* section of Wrangell-St. Elias allows anyone with a gun and an Alaska state hunting license to sport hunt. The definition of a national preserve is, ironically, areas in which Congress has permitted continued public hunting, trapping, oil/gas exploration and extraction. Until this Alaska trip, Matt and I thought national preserves *protected* the land, its resources, and the animals that lived there. I guess the word *preserve* threw us off.

We took the other road into the park today, the infamous McCarthy Road, which starts on the east side of the park at the town of Chitina and runs for 60 miles to the towns of Kennecott and McCarthy. Kennecott is a former mining town restored and maintained by the park service. When copper was discovered in the area in 1900, the Kennecott Mining Company built the mines and the company town of Kennecott. Because alcohol and prostitution were forbidden in Kennecott, people in the nearby town of McCarthy sensed a lucrative business opportunity and built a bar and a brothel. Business was brisk, and McCarthy quickly grew. The Copper River and Northwestern Railway reached McCarthy in 1911. By 1938, however, the copper deposits in Kennecott Mountain were exhausted, people abandoned the towns, and the railroad discontinued service that year. McCarthy and Kennecott became ghost towns nearly overnight, and the population fell to almost zero until the area became a national park.

The park service website calls the road to McCarthy "An Alaskan Adventure!" People who have driven it say it's the worst road in America. It usually takes three hours to drive the length of the road one way. Other hazards can make it longer: heavy rain, giant potholes, washboard ruts and large, sharp rocks. The road follows the abandoned railroad track, and you can see evidence of that when you cross the bridge at Mile 17. It was originally built in 1910 as a railroad bridge and is still used today to get cars and trucks across the raging Kuskulana River, 238 feet below.

Five miles into the drive, Matt determined that we were averaging about ten miles per hour, so at that rate it would take six hours to get to McCarthy. Eventually, the road smoothed out, and we were able to make it up to 35 miles an hour. It felt like we were flying. We didn't see any wildlife from the road, but there were great views of the surrounding mountains. When we got to the rickety narrow bridge over the Lakina River, there was a state road worker on each side, stopping every car. They told us that the bridge would close at 5pm, and whatever side of the bridge we were on at that time was the side we would be on until the bridge reopened at 9am the next morning. Thank you, good to know.

McCarthy Road ends at a parking lot where you must leave your car, walk the final quarter of a mile, and cross a footbridge over the Kennicott River to get to McCarthy. On the other side of the footbridge, you can walk to McCarthy or take a shuttle to Kennecott, five miles away. When we got out of the car, we saw a shuttle van sitting on the other side of the footbridge and assumed it was the shuttle to Kennicott, which runs every half hour. I could see Matt's head swiveling back and forth, judging the distance to the shuttle against the baggage he had with him - me. He said, "We can make it!" Then he sprinted shouting, "Run, Karen, run!" We ran like maniacs; our backpacks bouncing, and us waving and yelling, "Wait, wait!" to the shuttle driver. We got there just in time, panting and sweating, and piled in with the other passengers. The van pulled away, two minutes later it stopped, and everyone got off. Matt and I looked at each other and laughed. We ran like crazy people to catch a half-mile ride when we could have easily walked. Shortly thereafter, a different shuttle took us to Kennecott.

Kennecott was buzzing with construction activity. Listed on the National Register of Historic Places in 1978, and designated as a National Historic Landmark since 1986, Kennecott is considered the best remaining example of early 20th Century copper mining. Many of the buildings in Kennecott were abandoned for 70 years. The National Park Service had to identify which buildings to stabilize or rehabilitate, and which ones could not be saved. Their goal was to protect the town's historic integrity, while rehabilitating a few buildings for the park service and the public to use. The Recreation Hall, used for educational programs and community events, was completed in 2004. The Store and Post Office serves as the visitor center. It looks today like the general store must have looked 100 years ago, complete with canned goods on the shelves. Other buildings are currently receiving repairs to roofs, foundations and walls. The stabilization work, which can only be done during summer months, is expected to take many years.

Inside the Kennecott Visitor Center were rubber molds of animal tracks. There was a wolf, black bear and brown bear. The mold of the black bear paw was impressive, larger than Matt's hand. I picked up the mold of the brown bear (grizzly) paw. It was monstrous, like what I imagine a dinosaur paw would be. I shuddered to think of coming into contact with an animal that large in the wilderness. When we left the visitor center to begin our hike, I took the package of salmon jerky that I had in my backpack out and threw it away. If bears that large were in Wrangell, I didn't want to hike through the woods smelling like a giant piece of smoked salmon.

As we hiked from Kennecott to Root Glacier, a four-mile round trip, we could hear the land to our left cracking and moaning. We couldn't figure out what the noise was. The sound was coming from what looked like a gravel patch, which was a mile wide and several miles long. We didn't realize it was part of a glacier until later when we saw layers of ice underneath the gravel and grit. The trail led to the edge of Root Glacier where we stood and gazed at the vast expanse of packed snow and ice.

It was tempting to walk out onto the glacier, but we didn't have the right equipment or training. There are many things in Alaska that can kill you; a glacier is one of them.

Crevasses and icefalls make glaciers deadly. A crevasse is an open break or cut in the surface of the glacier. You could fall in and never be seen again. Toward the end of the summer, crevasses are at their widest, and they are covered with the least amount of snow. Snow bridges form on top of crevasses and add to the danger because they look solid, but they're just a thin covering over a deep hole. One wrong step and you could break through. An icefall is the steep part of a glacier that often looks like a frozen waterfall. Glaciers are always moving slowly; the movement causes stress, which leads to cracking, which causes blocks of ice to break off and tumble. Sometimes an entire section of the icefall front collapses; you don't want to be standing too close when that happens. At Kennecott, there are wilderness guides who provide visitors with the proper equipment and take them out onto Root Glacier. Since Matt and I were on our own, we were happy to admire it from a distance.

After we had gotten back to the visitor center, we took the shuttle to McCarthy and strolled through the tiny town before returning to our car. The park literature says that McCarthy is the "last remaining remote intact community of individuals inside a national park." This community of about 50 residents includes a couple of hotels, a saloon, gift store, liquor store and a hardware/grocery store. The buildings had been historically restored to look like they did 100 years ago.

It was a long three-hour drive back on the McCarthy Road. I had been looking forward to eating the other bag of smoked salmon jerky we had left in the car, but as I pulled the top of the bag open, it exploded and salmon jerky flew everywhere. Some of the pieces went into the air-conditioning and heating vents. Whoever rents this car in the future will curiously find themselves craving smoked salmon. Coincidentally, about that time we saw a bear on the road. We tried to get a picture, but he was too far away. He disappeared into the forest before we could pull closer.

Once out of the park and headed back toward Copper Center, we stopped for dinner at a local pizza restaurant. The place was empty except for two other people who also sat in the bar. On my way to the bathroom, I walked through the main room of the restaurant, which was once a garage, and almost tripped over a man who looked to be 100 years old, in his pajamas, and asleep in a lawn chair in front of a giant TV. When I came back to the bar I told Matt what I saw, but he didn't believe me. A few minutes later, we heard a loud, "I can't get this remote to work!" Matt turned around to see Mr. Pajama Man, with a dirty Santa Claus beard, standing at the bar waving the remote. The owner muttered something and went off into the garage area with the old guy, returning a minute later still muttering.

We ordered a sausage and jalapeno pizza like we always do. The pizza came out on a rusted, dented and what may have been a panning-for-gold pan. The sausage looked like chopped hotdog, and the jalapeños weren't on top of the pizza, they were cold and in a separate bowl. The owner of the restaurant, Vicky, kept calling them "ha-la-peen-as." She said, "I never know how many ha-la-peen-as people want on their pizza, so I just leave them on the side." After she left Matt said to me quietly, "Wouldn't that be true for *any* pizza topping?" (Matt was so amused with the way she pronounced jalapeños that he kept using the word in conversation as often as he could, and mispronouncing it the way she did.) It was the worst restaurant pizza we'd ever had; we've had worse freezer burn pizza at home, but that would be an unfair comparison. Not wanting to hurt Vicky's feelings, I tried to eat my fair share, but I couldn't. I looked around to see if there was a dog we could feed it to under the table. In Alaska, it seems there's a dog always hanging around these local restaurants and taverns. No dog. I glanced hopefully back at the old man in his pajamas. He was asleep again.

Vicky kept walking by our table, making comments like "You're sure not eating very much." Matt and I finally managed to choke down a piece and asked her to wrap up the rest "for later." When we got back to our hotel room, we put the rest of the pizza in our trashcan. Whoever checks into this room tomorrow is going to think the room smells like hotdogs and ha-la-peen-as instead of old-lady perfume.

Your Friend,
Karen

From: **Matt Smith**
Subject: **Driving to Denali**
Date: **August 24, 2010**

Dear Bob & Sue,

Every road sign in Alaska has bullet holes. Even the new ones; the manufacturers must send them from the factory with a starter hole or two. I realized, as I was driving along the highway today, that the Alaska state flag is a blue road sign with bullet holes in the pattern of the Big Dipper.

We had three options for getting to Denali. First, we could backtrack toward Anchorage then turn north on Parks Highway (Parks Highway is named after George Parks, former governor of the Alaska Territory; it's not named Parks Highway because it leads to Denali National Park, which it does). Our second option was to go north from Copper Center on Highway 4 and then turn west on the Denali Highway (which is named after Denali). This looked to be the most direct route, however, the Denali Highway is 135 miles in length and more than 100 miles of it is unpaved. After driving the 60-mile unpaved McCarthy Road yesterday – twice – I couldn't pull the trigger on that option. Third we could drive to Fairbanks and then turn south on the Parks Highway, following it to Denali. That's the route we chose.

The scenery on the drive to Fairbanks was beautiful; the highway crosses the Alaska Range of mountains. There is so much wilderness in Alaska that it's easy to imagine there are entire mountain ranges that no one has explored. Very few cars were on the highway, and in the middle of the range, we stopped to take pictures of glaciers that were just a mile or so from the road. A fox crossed 50 yards in front of us. Alaska is a beautiful place.

We knew we were getting back to civilization when we came to a nice little town north of the mountains that had three gas stations, two liquor stores and a road sign with no bullet holes. The sign was in a school zone; instead of bullet holes it had paint gun splatters. Seriously, I'm not making this up.

In Fairbanks, we stopped for lunch, and then continued south toward Denali. The drive south from Fairbanks to Denali was not as interesting as the drive this morning. For much of the way, trees block the view from the highway making it impossible to get a sense of the surrounding country.

South of Fairbanks, Karen was car weary and slaphappy. We passed a billboard for Skinny Dicks Halfway Inn; this became her entertainment for a good 50 miles. She worked "Skinny Dick" into our conversation as many times as possible. I was relieved when we passed a dead skunk on the side of the road hoping it would break the pattern. Karen said nothing for about two minutes then asked me if I thought Skinny Dick had hit that skunk with his car. I muttered, "Please Lord, let Denali be over the next hill."

By late afternoon we were at the entrance to Denali National Park. We took care of business, and picked up our tickets for tomorrow; we're taking a bus 66 miles to the Eielson Visitor Center in the center of the park.

Your Friend,
Matt

From: **Matt Smith**
Subject: **#13 – Denali National Park**
Date: **August 25, 2010**

Dear Bob & Sue,

Our shuttle bus to Eielson Visitor Center left at 8:30am. The trip took four hours one-way. Usually we avoid organized tours, but the general public is not allowed to drive past the ranger checkpoint at mile 15 of the park road. If you want to see anything beyond that point, you have to take a bus or walk.

We only had one day scheduled to go into the park, and we didn't want to miss our bus. All the shuttle times were sold out, so taking a later bus was not an option. People started lining up 20 minutes early for each bus.

While we were in line, an older man (older than us) walked out of the transit building and past the lines for the buses. He stood in the middle of the road and shouted, "Where's our bus!" Then he shouted toward the transit building for his wife, "Nancy!" A minute later, he shouted again, "Nancy!" Finally, Nancy came out; she was struggling to put on her coat and wrestling a large bag carrying the items she purchased at the gift shop. "Nancy, where's our bus!"

"I don't know where our bus is!" (I don't think they were aware they were shouting.)

"Well it's supposed to be right here!"

The old guy walked over to the worker who was coordinating the loading of buses. He shouted, "Where's our bus!"

"Sir, what bus do you have tickets for?"

"Eight o'clock!"

"It's 8:20 sir." The old guy looked at the worker like he didn't hear him. "Your bus is probably already gone, sir."

"Well it's supposed to be right here! Nancy! Where's our bus!"

"I don't know where our bus is!"

This went on for a while. I'm pretty sure they spent the rest of the day in the gift shop.

There are two types of buses that go into the park: tour buses (that are narrated with lunch provided) and shuttle buses. We took one of the shuttle buses, which are not narrated, but our driver shared some interesting park information with us. Once the shuttle bus is past mile marker 15, you can get off wherever you want and then catch another shuttle later. To allow for this, they save a few empty seats on each bus. The busses run about every 15 minutes.

Some people take the shuttle into the park, get off and hike for hours then come back to the road and catch the next shuttle that comes by. The shuttle buses are for people who are more self-sufficient; you bring your own food and water and plan your own itinerary. It was nice for me not to have to drive, so I could look out at the scenery and wildlife instead of the road.

Once we passed the ranger checkpoint, we felt like we were really in the park. Everyone on the bus was looking for wildlife, except the couple in the row across from us. They were eating. They ate continuously. The wife would pull out a sandwich bag full of nuts, eat one nut, give her husband one nut and then put the bag away. She'd get a granola bar out, take one small bite, give it to her husband, so he could take one small bite, and then put it away. She'd rummage around for another bag, eat one carrot and put it away. Non-stop. Apple slices, potato chips, sandwiches, cookies. I never saw them eating the same thing twice, but they were always eating. They never looked out the windows.

About an hour into our trip, John our bus driver stopped when he spotted a bear. It was a mother bear with two cubs. They were maybe a half-mile away up the hillside. I'm glad Karen and I both brought binoculars on this trip. In Alaska, you need binoculars or a good telephoto lens on your camera to see much of the wildlife. The bears were grizzlies, but smaller than the coastal bears that live close by the ocean. The coastal bears have evolved into much larger animals because of their diet of salmon. The bears in Denali are mostly vegetarian; berries are their main food.

The park ranger we spoke with at the visitor center had a relaxed attitude about the bears in the park. She said if we don't bother them, they won't bother us. This was much different from the bear warnings we got in Glacier Bay, where bear spray is advised on all hikes, and trails are frequently closed because of bear activity. Still, if you ever run into a grizzly bear in the wild the main difference to remember is the larger bears can kill you in about two seconds while it takes the smaller bears about three seconds. In total, we saw ten bears today; three sightings of a mother with two cubs and one lone bear.

The park road past mile marker 15 is gravel but well maintained. The main reason it takes four hours to get to Eielson is because of the stops for wildlife sightings and bathroom breaks. At our first bathroom stop, we overheard a woman complaining to John our driver. She said, "Can we skip the bathroom and wildlife stops? I just want to get there." John was very polite but explained that people come to the park to see wildlife and no, we can't skip the bathroom stops. I wondered where she thought "there" was; we were "there."

Very soon after we pulled out of the rest area, John stopped the bus in the road. I could hear the complainer exhale loudly. There was a wolf pup in the road ahead. John thought the pup was born this spring. He wasn't very big, but he had huge paws. We all looked for the other members of the pack, but couldn't find them. I'm sure they were very close by.

I looked over at the couple that had been eating to see if they had any interest in seeing the wolf pup. They were both asleep with their mouths open.

John our driver looked like he was about 70 years old. He told us at the beginning of the trip to yell, "Stop!" when we saw wildlife because the engine noise was loud, and he couldn't hear us unless we yelled. This started a very annoying pattern of "Stops!" that lasted all morning. There were many false alarms and sightings of animals so far away we would have needed the Hubble telescope to see them. At a curve in the road, the bus came very close to the edge of a cliff. I was sitting in the window seat on the cliff side of the bus. Looking straight down, I couldn't see any part of the road, only fluorescent cones that once marked the edge of the road, which had fallen several hundred feet to the bottom of the valley. I was hoping no one would yell, "Stop!" at that moment; it wouldn't be a good time to frighten or distract John.

When we arrived at the Eielson Visitor Center, we ate our lunch outside. Sadly Mt. McKinley wasn't "out." Because of frequent cloud cover, only about 30 percent of visitors to Denali see Mt. McKinley. So many visitors miss seeing the mountain that inside the visitor center, on a large window that frames a view of the mountain, the park service drew the silhouette of Mount McKinley. There is a spot on the floor where you can stand, and if your eye level is just right and you look at the drawing on the window, that's where the mountain would be.

After lunch, we hiked the Alpine Trail behind the visitor center. The hike was a 1,000-foot elevation gain and one mile long. At the top, there was a 360-degree view of the park. The hike was steep, but it felt good since we'd been sitting all morning. We got some amazing pictures at the top.

Because of our hike, we missed the return departure of our original bus, so we had to catch another shuttle back to the park entrance. However, one of the shuttles had broken down, so the people who would have been on it were now also waiting to get on another shuttle. We had to put our name on a waiting list, and wait through several buses to catch a ride. There were about 30 people in our same situation standing around with us.

Everyone was relieved when finally an empty bus arrived that could take us back. The waiting list "manager," who clearly was having a bad day, started calling out names to board the bus. He called out, "Kim, party of three." No response. He yelled louder, "Kim!" Again, no response. He looked around the parking lot and in the visitor center, then came back to the bus. One more time he called out, "Kim!" Suddenly, we heard voices and saw hands waving out of the windows of the broken down bus. The Kim family had been sitting in the back of the broken down bus ready to go. Everyone, including the Kims laughed, which broke the tension. The manager waved them over to the new bus; he shook his head and said, "Now *that* was funny."

The shuttle makes fewer stops on its way back to the park entrance. The bar is higher for wildlife sightings in the afternoon because everyone is bus weary. Park regulations say you must stay at least a quarter of a mile away from large wildlife. But, for practical reasons, if a bus stops and wildlife approaches it, the bus doesn't have to back up.

On the way back to the entrance, our bus came around a blind curve and about 100 feet in front of us was a group of Dall Sheep in the road. The bus driver stopped the bus and turned off the engine. We sat there for about 15 minutes as the sheep ate and ambled toward our bus. They walked right past the bus, and then down the mountainside. We had a front row seat. It was fun to see them so close; usually you see mountain sheep as tiny specks miles away on a cliff.

It was a great day in the park; I'm sure we'll be back someday. Tomorrow we head south to Seward, Alaska.

Your Friend,
Matt

From: **Karen Smith**
Subject: **#14 – Kenai Fjords National Park**
Date: **August 26, 2010**

Dear Bob & Sue,

It's nice to start the day with the smell of three-day old smoked salmon jerky. As we left for Seward bright and early in our rental car, the smell came blowing out of the heating vents. When the salmon jerky bag exploded in Wrangell-St. Elias, salmon bits flew into crevices so small that the only way to get them out would be to dismantle the dashboard. Good thing it's a rental.

Kenai Fjords National Park is one of only three national parks in Alaska that you can drive to. About 100 miles south of Anchorage, it covers 1,760 sq. miles of the Kenai Peninsula near the town of Seward, the park's headquarters. Kenai Fjords National Park was created in 1980 to protect the scenic and environmental integrity of the Harding Icefield, its glaciers and the coastal fjords, islands, and peninsulas of the Kenai coast.

We didn't see much of that scenic beauty today when we arrived in Seward; it was dreary, raining and the clouds were low. After checking into our hotel along the harbor, we walked to the Information Center down the street. Matt struck up a conversation with a ranger, asking her about other things to do in the park besides the boat tour. (We're doing that tomorrow.) The ranger asked if we were bird watchers. Matt said, "No." There was an uncomfortable silence; Matt felt like he needed to explain, "We don't have anything against birds; we just aren't that interested - we don't have a life list of birds." A woman looking at postcards next to me overheard the conversation and started laughing at Matt. If I had a nickel for every time...

We drove to the Exit Glacier area, the only part of the park accessible by road. Exit Glacier is open year-round, but once it starts snowing, usually in mid-November, the road is closed to cars until weather permitting in May. **During those months,** you would need a snow machine or dogsled to get there, unless you want to snowshoe or cross-country ski the 8.6 miles from Seward Highway to the Exit Glacier parking lot. Exit Glacier is a half-mile wide river of ice, one of 30 glaciers flowing outward from the 700-square-mile Harding Icefield. There's a hiking trail that goes to the edge of the glacier, as well as a strenuous four-mile trail up to the Harding Icefield.

As soon as we entered the park's boundary, we stopped and took our picture in front of the Kenai Fjords National Park sign. The decrepit condition of the sign shocked me – it had peeling paint and what looked like bullet holes. As the first thing visitors see when they enter the park, you can't underestimate the importance of the park sign. We may seem like geeks because we're thrilled when we see a park sign, but we're not the only ones. Many people have told us that they get excited when they're driving into the park and first glimpse the sign; for others, it brings back memories of childhood vacations. For as long as the parks have existed, families have pulled up in their touring cars, station wagons, mini-vans and SUVs to take their photo in front of the sign.

Every national park sign is unique, and most reflect something special about their park, either on the sign itself or in the local materials used to build it. In its current condition, the Kenai Fjords sign appears to be welcoming visitors to a shooting range. I know park budgets are tight, but with a couple of volunteers, some wood-filler and a can of paint, this sign could once again proudly welcome visitors to the park. I'm going to mention this on the Kenai Fjords comments card and send it to the superintendent.

We strolled through the Exit Glacier Nature Center looking at the exhibits, and checked out the Alaska Geographic bookstore. When we got back to the car, Matt realized he had mistakenly picked up a Bear Safety brochure instead of the park map. He went back in to get his own map because I will no longer share mine. We decided early in our parks trip that in order to avoid unnecessary bickering we should get two maps and newsletters at every park. Matt puts the unopened, pristine map and newsletter away in his file, and I'm free to do with mine whatever I like: wrinkle it, tear it, stain it, use it as a sun shield on long car rides, level wobbly tables in restaurants, re-fold it incorrectly or use it as a napkin. Matt calls my maps "biohazards." So, I'm not sharing.

Back in our hotel room, Matt told me about his Photo of the Day Contest. I laughed but I shouldn't have. It was just so cute and slightly pathetic. Matt is the one who takes the photos; Matt is the only one who enters photos into the contest, and Matt is the one who decides which photo is the winner. The way it works is this: he downloads all the day's photos onto his laptop. He looks through them and then selects the top three. He moves the three finalists onto his desktop, studies them again, thinks about it for awhile, and then chooses a winner which gets to appear in the "Photo of the Day" spot on our website.

I mentioned to him that I'd like to be one of the judges of the Photo of the Day, but his feelings were hurt because I had laughed at him. He said, "I don't think you're the kind of judge we are looking for at this time."

Who's "we?"

After walking through Seward's downtown and not finding any place that met all Matt's dining requirements – no bright lights, no bad live music, no strong smells of cleaning fluid, no Formica eating surfaces and no screaming children – we ended up back in the harbor area at the bar of a seafood restaurant.

We sat at the bar and ate seafood chowder. It was fantastic. The bartender turned to the guy sitting next to Matt and asked, "How big?" The guy replied, "187 pounds." That was the weight of the halibut he had caught today. I guess that's a good catch; he had the biggest steak on the menu in front of him and was eating like he hadn't seen food in a week.

After one beer and chowder, we called it a night; we have a long day tomorrow with the boat tour.

Your Friend,
Karen

From: **Karen Smith**
Subject: **Kenai Fjords boat tour**
Date: **August 27, 2010**

Dear Bob & Sue,

We have good news and bad news to report about our boat tour of Kenai Fjords National Park. The bad news is the weather today was rainy and foggy, and since we'd already bought non-refundable tickets we were going no matter what. The good news is that often when it rains there are seas of 15-20 ft. and 30-40 mph winds, but today the ocean was calm, so we weren't puking over the side of the boat. That's where they ask you to puke so you don't clog the toilets. They call it "feeding the fish."

The best way to see a big chunk of the park and its wildlife is by boat. There are several boat tours to choose from, all run by private concessionaires. We went with the 8-hour cruise, which included lunch and an all-you-can-eat salmon and prime rib dinner on Fox Island with a park ranger presentation. There was, however, no park ranger on board our boat. Our tickets cost $164 each, which we thought was pricey. It seems like that price would be out of reach for most families, which may explain why there were so few children on board.

We didn't see any whales or bears today, but I'm sure they were out there. At some spots, it was too foggy to see anything farther than 50 feet from the boat. We did see Dall's porpoises, Steller sea lions, harbor seals and sea otters. We saw a sea otter close to our boat eating an octopus. That was creepy watching it tear off arms of the octopus and eat them like stalks of celery. Otters are the largest members of the weasel family, but they are adorable (when they're not ripping apart the other animals) floating around on their backs. A ranger told us the cutest thing; to keep from drifting apart when they sleep, sometimes they hold paws.

The highlight of the tour was seeing the Aialik Glacier, the largest tidewater glacier in the park, which comes off of the Harding Icefield. It's hard to describe how tiny the boat suddenly seemed when the engine stopped, and we were bobbing next to the immense blue cliff of ice that was cracking and falling into the sea with thunderous sounds.

Even though the weather was bad, the boat was warm, the seats were comfortable, and we would have just settled back and enjoyed looking out the window except - the captain wouldn't stop talking. Since there wasn't a park ranger on board, he was our tour guide. On our Glacier Bay boat tour ranger Jane was informative while still being professional and respectful of where we were, a national park – a wilderness area. The captain of our boat today *really* liked the sound of his voice. Now, I agree enthusiasm is good, but he came off like a cheesy Las Vegas lounge performer – on an eight-hour shift. There was nowhere on the boat we could go to get away from the sound of his voice. "Allrighty folks, now sit tight and hold on to your seats! You are about to see (his voice drops to a dramatic whisper) a........black.......billed.......magpie."

The captain was clearly a birder. He maneuvered the boat in and around the Chiswell Islands, home to countless birds: horned and tufted puffins, thick-billed murres, black-legged kittiwakes and auklets to name a few. The captain was explaining the nesting habits of the tufted puffin when he stopped, handed his microphone to some unlucky passenger and made him say, "Picture perfect puffins" ten times fast. Spit flew, and Matt got out his iPod and headphones to drown out the sound.

The last straw came at the end of the tour as the boat was making its way toward Fox Island for dinner. "Do you want to add a half pound of crab to your all-you-can-eat salmon and prime rib dinner for $8?" They asked us that question when we bought our tickets online, and they asked us again when we picked up our tickets this morning at the boat dock. No thanks. We were already planning to eat $164 worth of salmon and prime rib. Still, the Captain got on the loudspeaker to let us know that this was our last and final chance to purchase this incredible deal. Only $8.00! He added, "This is Alaskan crab, not Russian crab." On top of being annoyed, we then wondered what the difference was between Alaskan and Russian crab.

Then he left the wheel and went around the boat. He stopped at every table to make a personal plea to add a half-pound of crab to the all-you-can-eat salmon and prime rib dinner. What I wanted to know was, while the captain was hawking crab, who was steering the boat?

Despite having missed out on the Alaskan crab (not Russian crab), the lodge on Fox Island was beautiful, and the food was excellent. We stuffed ourselves with salmon, but when the boat dropped us back at the Seward dock it was only 6:00pm, so we went back to the same bar as last night for more seafood chowder.

The waitress recognized us and said, "You missed all the excitement last night." After we had left, a black bear lumbered down the pier outside the restaurant and walked beside the boats, sniffing and poking around. Then he walked along the deck right outside the windows of the restaurant. The restaurant called the police, and they took the bear away. They had to put him down; he was a repeat offender, and this was his final strike.

Matt was tired by the end of the day. Maybe it was the Dramamine he had taken earlier, or maybe it was the effect of our long trip and a lot of driving. He said to me, "Trying to visit all 58 parks in such a short time feels like being in a hot dog eating contest. We're just trying to shove them down as fast as possible. We need to enjoy the journey and not make it a race." I agreed.

Tomorrow if the weather improves we are planning to hike to Exit Glacier, and possibly the Harding Ice Field. After that we'll head toward Anchorage.

Your Friend,
Karen

From: **Matt Smith**
Subject: **#15 – Crater Lake National Park**
Date: **September 6, 2010**

Dear Bob and Sue,

After Labor Day, it's walkers and strollers season in the national parks. The crowds are smaller, and the prices are lower, and it's the perfect time to start a 13-park road trip. Families with school-aged children have wrapped up their summer vacations, and it's just old people and babies (except for us, we're neither).

Yesterday we drove from Issaquah to Roseburg, Oregon. We got an inexpensive motel room in Roseburg because Crater Lake Lodge was sold out. Karen isn't a big fan of motels where the front door of the room opens to the parking lot. She makes me sleep on the side of the bed closest to the window, so "the bullets will hit me first" when the shooting starts.

So, you can imagine how uncomfortable she was last night, as we were unloading our car outside our room, and she's standing next to a man with no pants. We think he was staying in the room next door. He was searching for something in the trunk of his car for a very long time, with nothing on below the waist, nothing. We think he was looking for his pants.

No bullets or naked men came into our room last night, so we were well rested this morning for our drive to Crater Lake National Park. We got to the park about 10:30am. There was not a cloud in the sky, but a haze from an active forest fire hung in the air. It was a small fire, but it had been burning for a couple of weeks and was not actively being suppressed.

We entered the park through the north entrance and drove east on the rim road around the crater stopping at several overlooks. On a sunny day like today, the color of the lake looks unreal; it's a stunning blue. Crater Lake is one of those places like the Grand Canyon that everyone should see in their lifetime. This is our second trip to the park. Last September, we spent a long weekend here when we were fortunate enough to get a room in the lodge. That's also something everyone should do once; stargazing on the back patio of the lodge while looking over the lake is awe-inspiring.

Just to the east of the crater is Mount Scott, the highest point in the park at 8,926 feet. There's a five-mile round-trip hike to the summit where a lookout tower sits. It's a moderate hike with an elevation gain of 1,250 feet. We parked near the trailhead and hiked to the summit.

I have a small voice recorder I use for taking notes that I carry with me almost all the time. It's easier to use the recorder than to write notes, especially while on a hike. Halfway to the summit of Mount Scott, Karen took my voice recorder from me. She wanted to make a formal complaint for the record.

Her complaints were numerous: a) She feels that I trick her into going on strenuous hikes. b) I falsely promise to go slowly and stop to for rest breaks. c) I never stop to take in the beauty of the surroundings. (She referred to our hikes as "death marches".) d) I ignore her gasping and wheezing. e) Finally, I never look back to make sure she is OK, or that a bear hasn't gotten her.

Bob and Sue, this is your fault, of course. Whenever we go for hikes with you, Karen notices how you hold hands the entire way. She thinks *we* should hold hands on our hikes, and kiss every now and then. You guys are getting me in trouble.

I got the recorder back from Wheezy, and we made it to the summit in about half the time the park newsletter says it should take. The views were amazing. We had a good view of the fire from the summit. It wasn't large, but it put out a large amount of smoke. The lake was almost mirror flat; the only ripples were the ones made by the tour boat going to Wizard Island.

After the hike, we made peanut butter and jelly sandwiches in the back seat of our car. We realized before this trip that we could save money by not eating in restaurants and snack bars for every meal. Also, when we were here a year ago I had a bad experience with my lunch from the snack bar. I was halfway through my sandwich when the top piece of bread fell off. There was an iridescent rainbow on my roast beef. I like rainbows as much as the next guy, just not on my meat. In defense of the snack bar, I don't think the meat was spoiled. I never got sick, but still...

We finished lunch and drove the rim road toward Crater Lake Lodge, then out of the park through the same entrance we came in this morning. Tonight we are staying at Homewood Suites in Medford. We've never stayed at a Homewood Suites before, so we didn't know that dinner was included in the price of the room. The woman checking us in told us that dinner would be served from 5:30-7:30pm, the menu was hamburgers and hotdogs, and as always, free beer and wine. Karen said, "It's our lucky day. They have our two favorite things, beer and free."

Your Friend,
Matt

From: **Matt Smith**
Subject: **#16 – Redwood National Park**
Date: **September 7, 2010**

Dear Bob and Sue,

Karen is a banana smuggler. On our drive from Medford, Oregon to Arcata, California today we stopped to hike in Redwood National Park. At the California border, I lied to the agriculture inspector who asked if we had any produce in our car. I said we didn't, but Karen had a banana in her purse. I tried to get it from her before we got to the inspection station, but she said she would "never give it up." By lying to the inspector, I became an accomplice. I don't even like bananas.

Karen tried to justify her actions by saying bananas aren't produce. Then she gave me her personal guarantee that her banana didn't have any diseases or insects, *and* it posed no danger to California's agriculture industry. As soon as we pulled out of sight of the inspection station, I made her eat it, so we would be legal again. I should have turned her in at the border.

Karen always has a banana with her when we travel. She says it's the perfect travel fruit; it will always be clean on the inside when she's ready to eat it. A few years ago we were in London and took a day trip to Windsor Castle. The Queen was in residence, so security was tighter than normal. The guards searched Karen's purse. Can you guess what they pulled out? A banana. They put the banana on the conveyor belt to be X-rayed. The guards gathered around and laughed as the banana slid beneath the X-ray curtain. One of the guards said, "Look, the banana's going to see Mum."

Once across the California border, we entered what we thought was Redwood National Park. At the Prairie Creek Visitor Center, we found a person who we thought was a volunteer ranger, and asked his suggestion for a two to three-hour moderate hike in the national park. He gave us an unpleasant look and asked, "Why do you want to hike in the *national* park?" That seemed like an odd question. I explained how we are visiting all the national parks, and we would like to hike in Redwood National Park. He rolled his eyes and said, "OK, but the trails in the state park are *much* better." He gave us a map and highlighted several hikes we should consider. They were all in the state park. Later we realized that Prairie Creek Visitor Center is in one of the units of Redwood State Park that are clustered around Redwood National Park.

There's seems to be a strained rivalry between Redwood State Park and Redwood National Park. A national park ranger told us that when the law was passed to create the *national* park it called for all the state park land along the coast in northwest California to be included in Redwood National Park. The state wasn't happy about this so not all the old state park land was included in the national park. We didn't get a clear answer when we asked how the state was able *not* to comply with the federal mandate. Now that California is having budget problems, they want the federal government to help with resources to manage Redwood State Park. At least that's what we were told. We just wanted to take a cool hike among the coastal redwoods, not get in the middle of a senseless squabble between government agencies.

Regardless, we made sure that at least part of our hike went through the national park, so we're *official.* Tomorrow we are driving to Redding, California and will visit Lassen Volcanic National Park the next day.

Wish you guys were with us.

Your Friend,
Matt

From: **Matt Smith**
Subject: **#17 – Lassen Volcanic National Park**
Date: **September 9, 2010**

Dear Bob and Sue,

We had no wildlife sightings today in Lassen Volcanic National Park; we saw lots of squirrels, but Karen said they don't count as wildlife. She gets frustrated when I repeatedly stop our hikes to take pictures of small animals - like squirrels and lizards. We agreed that from now on there would be a two-pound minimum weight requirement for any animal to qualify as a wildlife sighting. If I see an animal below that weight, I've agreed not shout, "Karen, look!" And, I will only stop to take their picture if I can do so without Karen having to break her stride. Birds are exempt from the weight minimum. If there's any doubt whether an animal meets the two-pound requirement, I will be the sole judge.

When we woke up this morning, it was a gloomy day. Karen suggested we go back to bed; skip the park, and tell everyone we visited it anyway. She said, "No one will know. If someone asks us what the park was like we'll say, 'The trees and mountains were beautiful, it was a magical place, yada yada yada.' You can move some of your squirrel pictures from the other parks into the Lassen file folder and no one will ever know we didn't go." Later she said she regretted her suggestion and asked me not to tell anyone. I assured her it would be our secret.

It took more than an hour to drive from Redding to the southwest entrance of the park; we got to the Kohm Yah-mah-nee Visitor Center about 9:00am. The park and the visitor center are open year-round, but because of the amount of snow Lassen receives each year, the main park road past the visitor center is usually closed from October through June, sometimes as late as July. The temperature was 36 when we arrived, with frost in most places and a couple inches of snow at the higher elevations. The snow would be gone within an hour after we arrived, but we were able to get a few good photos before it melted.

Our first hike was the Bumpass Hell Trail, which has the largest concentration of hydrothermal features in the park: boiling mudpots, fumaroles and steaming pools. It looks like a small version of Yellowstone. The sun broke through the clouds as we got to the boardwalk that allows you to walk over the thermally active areas. With the cold temperatures, bright sun and steam coming out of the ground, we got some great photos.

A *Good Morning America* cameraman (Burt) was there with a park ranger filming a segment about the park for the show. He asked if he could interview us about our impressions of the park. It took Karen about two seconds (maybe three) to brush her hair and put on lipstick using the back of her 68-cent bottle opener as a mirror. He said we might be on *Good Morning America* in a few weeks when they air the story. I hope in our first and most-likely last media interview we don't look like complete morons.

After finishing with Burt, we headed to the Lassen Peak trailhead parking lot. Lassen Peak is the southernmost active volcano in the Cascade Range. It exploded in 1915, and that eruption was the last one in the Cascades until Mt. St. Helens blew in 1980. The trail to the top of Lassen Peak is 2.5 miles one way. The summit provides spectacular views of the 1915 devastated area, but we only got to see part of the view. The park service closed the trail just past the halfway point to allow maintenance crews to work on stabilizing the upper half. Earlier in the season a falling rock struck and killed a young boy who was hiking on the trail with his family.

We then drove to the Summit Lake South campgrounds, and from there hiked two miles to Echo Lake, the first lake on the Cluster Lakes Loop. We were surprised at how beautiful and pristine the park was; a park that we'd never even heard of a year ago. Karen called it a "hidden gem." It's every bit as spectacular as the more popular national parks, but without traffic jams and crowds of people. We nearly had the place to ourselves.

Driving north on the main park road we left the park through the northwest gate, and headed back to Redding where we're staying again tonight. Tomorrow we're driving to Yosemite.

Your Friend,
Matt

From: **Matt Smith**
Subject: **#18 – Yosemite National Park**
Date: **September 10, 2010**

Dear Bob and Sue,

Yosemite has been on Karen's "must see before I die" list for a long time. Her head was hanging out the window as we entered the park from the northwest, at the Big Oak Flat Entrance. We stopped and took our picture by the park sign, and then drove into the valley for our first look. After everything we'd read and heard about this "crown jewel" of the park system, we wondered if it would live up to the hype. Yosemite Falls was dry (in September water levels are too low for the falls to flow), but even without the famous waterfall spilling over the canyon walls, the valley was every bit as spectacular as promised.

Today was our "getting the lay of the land day," which is what we do when we arrive in a park for the first time late in the afternoon. We take a look around, check out the food and beverage offerings, or lack thereof, take care of our park business and get suggestions from the park rangers about hikes to do the following day(s).

We drove through a giant parking lot in the middle of the valley. After squeezing into a parking spot between a couple of big-ass RVs, we walked past the bus stop and the lines of people waiting for the shuttle and continued on the paved path to the Yosemite Valley Visitor Center. It was surprising to see that Yosemite Village is a small city with lodging, restaurants, grocery store, deli, gift shops, post office, museum and a medical clinic. There were people everywhere.

We walked to the Ahwahnee Hotel to check it out. We have reservations there for our last night in the park. After I coaxed Karen out of the gift shop, we had a drink outside on the patio overlooking the back lawn. The weather was perfect, mid-70's and sunny.

Tonight we're staying at the Yosemite View Lodge just outside the west entrance to the park. We had a mishap on our hotel room balcony. While opening a beer, I dropped my 68-cent bottle opener. It bounced off our deck and landed on the roof of the room below us, out of reach. Fortunately, we have two backup 68-cent bottle openers, so we didn't have to try to bite the caps off. The best $2.04 I ever spent. Another good value were the $1.98 Sporks I bought for Karen and I. A Spork is a fork, spoon and knife all in one utensil. Karen cried when I gave it to her.

We're excited to hike and to see more of the park. Tomorrow we're headed up to the Tuolumne Meadows area.

Your Friend,
Matt

From: **Matt Smith**
Subject: **Yosemite day two**
Date: **September 11, 2010**

Dear Bob and Sue,

When we got to the parking area next to Lembert Dome this morning there were six deer in the meadow across Tioga Road. A couple of small ones were head-butting each other and kicking up dirt. It was fun to watch them play. Even Karen thought they were cute. Early on in our parks trip Karen said that deer aren't binocular-worthy because, "We see them at home all the time, most of the time dead along the side of the road." She said she would look at them if they come close enough to see with her naked eye.

Today we hiked to the Glen Aulin High Sierra Camp, our longest hike so far on this trip, 12.5 miles. The trail to Glen Aulin follows the Tuolumne River, which dumps into the Hetch Hetchy Reservoir 20 miles down stream. We hiked through alternating areas of shaded, cool forests and sunny patches of bare granite. The river was low, as it usually is in late summer. In several places, there were hikers jumping into the cold water. In the spring or early summer you couldn't do this without the current sweeping you down the river and over dangerous falls.

Stapled to the markers along the trail were signs asking people to be on the lookout for a missing hiker. He had failed to return to his camp when he said he would and was now several days late. About six miles into our hike, at a junction of two trails, rescue workers were questioning everyone who came by, trying to gather clues that might help them find the hiker. As crowded as these popular national parks can be, the wilderness is still vast, and people can get lost and disappear.

When we reached Glen Aulin, we were surprised to find a camp in the middle of the wilderness that provides tent cabins with real beds, hot showers and gourmet meals. Karen thought this might be the perfect way for her to "ease into the whole camping thing." She said she'd probably *love* to camp if she didn't have to carry a tent and a sleeping bag on her back, sleep on the cold, hard ground, eat freeze-dried food and pee in the woods. We were ready to sign up when she found out that the tents are dormitory style; you're assigned to a tent that sleeps either four women or four men. Goodnight John-Boy, goodnight Mary Ellen, goodnight Grandpa.

On our hike back to the car, the mule train that supplies the Glen Aulin camp passed us. Karen felt sorry for them. She said they looked sad, especially the little black one at the end of the train who was having trouble keeping up. I told her, "Of course they look sad, they're carrying hundreds of pounds of supplies on their backs so people like you can sleep in the wilderness in comfort and be fed gourmet meals."

After hiking back to our car, we drove 90 minutes to the Evergreen Lodge close to the Hetch Hetchy entrance of the park. We are staying here for two nights. The lodge was built in the 1920's to cater to the Hetch Hetchy Dam construction workers. Over the decades, various owners have added on to the resort. In the last ten years, the lodge has been renovated, and 75 new cabins were built. We're staying in one of the nice new cabins. My favorite spot in the complex is the tavern, which has 90 years of character, a big-screen TV showing college football and beer.

We just finished a great dinner and plan to hang out here, write down our notes from the day and download our pictures. Our hike today was beautiful and the weather perfect. We're glad we planned for several more days in Yosemite.

Your Friend,
Matt

From: **Karen Smith**
Subject: **Squirrels between our toes**
Date: **September 12, 2010**

Dear Bob and Sue,

We're back in the Evergreen Lodge tavern, and no, we haven't been here since last night. That wouldn't be a bad thing; they have sweet potato fries, and it's a great place to hang out. There's a wedding reception taking place in the courtyard off the restaurant, but at least a dozen of the male guests are here in the bar watching Sunday Night Football and cheering loudly. We're placing bets on whose wife stomps in here first to drag her husband away. The groom looks a little pissed off too. We can see his face through the window as he spins his mother around to a bad rendition of *You Are the Sunshine of My Life*.

Day three in Yosemite started with a drive to Glacier Point. It was a beautiful drive, but it's a long distance from the Evergreen Lodge, and it took much more time than we thought to get there due to winding roads and traffic. Glacier Point sits 3,214 feet above Yosemite Valley, providing great views of the entire valley, Half Dome and El Capitan.

Glacier Point was crowded with visitors today, many with expensive cameras. It was odd watching people take pictures of themselves in stupid poses. There was a park ranger stationed at the point, and visitors were taking their picture with her like she was a celebrity. A man with an elaborate camera on a huge tripod was taking pictures of the valley. He would point to a location and an assistant would carry the camera to that spot and set up the camera and tripod. The man would approach the camera; he would take the picture and then point to another location. The assistant would move the camera and tripod for him again. Very odd.

Starting at the Glacier Point parking lot, there's a 4.8-mile hike that leads down to Yosemite Valley. Matt wanted to do the hike, but we hadn't checked the park's shuttle schedule, so we weren't sure if we would get back to our car after the hike. I'm glad we didn't try it. I don't like hiking straight down; it bothers my knees. (I just sounded really old, didn't I?)

We saw a group of hikers in the parking lot obviously preparing to hike down to the valley. One of the hikers was standing upright and struggling to balance on one leg while stretching the other. Matt of course noticed his backpack. It looked way bigger than the hiker needed or could handle. This is something we see often in the parks, people who are over-geared and under-prepared.

From Glacier Point, we drove seven miles to the trailheads for both Sentinel Dome and Taft Point. The trails were crowded, and Matt had to shoehorn our car into the last available parking spot. Both hikes had amazing views. The elevation of Sentinel Dome is 8,122 feet, and from there, it's possible to see the Sierra Nevadas, Half Dome, Clouds Rest, Tenaya Canyon and The Giant Staircase. From Taft Point, there's a great view of Yosemite Valley and across the valley floor to El Capitan and Yosemite Falls (when it's flowing). One of the first things you see when you reach Taft Point is the Fissures. These are huge cracks in the granite with sheer 3,000-foot drop-offs and no guardrails. Not for the faint of heart.

There was a small squirrel poised on a rock at the edge of one of the fissures. It was motionless; it looked like a statue. Matt spent ten minutes trying to get just the right picture of it, even though we agreed that we would not stop a hike to photograph small animals.

As we reached the Fissures, we caught up with a youth group of about 50 kids hiking together. There didn't seem to be an adult in charge. The kids looked to be in their mid-teens. They were obviously having fun, but there was some serious grab-assing going on: throwing rocks, spitting, pretending to push someone off a cliff. It made Matt very nervous, so we turned around before we got to Taft Point. He didn't want to spend the rest of the day giving interviews to the park police if one of the teenagers ended up at the bottom of the 3,000-foot drop. Matt said he was glad to see that natural selection is still alive and well, but he didn't want to be an eyewitness to it.

This afternoon we drove into Yosemite Valley and walked to Curry Village. I couldn't believe the throngs of tourists staying in the cabins and tents. There's a pavilion in the village with a fireplace and free Wi-Fi where we were able to access the Internet. *Inside* the pavilion, squirrels were making themselves at home, scampering under the tables and between people's feet looking for food. It creeped me out. I couldn't concentrate; they kept popping up everywhere, so I left. I felt it was safer to wait for Matt outside, taking my chances that I could be crushed under tons of granite rock falling from Glacier Point like it did in 2008, than being in there with the squirrels.

Tonight is our last night at the Evergreen Lodge, tomorrow we're staying at the swanky Ahwahnee Hotel. Before we check-in, I need to scrape the mud off my hiking boots and scrub the toothpaste off my suitcase.

Your Friend,
Karen

From: **Karen Smith**
Subject: **Yosemite day four**
Date: **September 13, 2010**

Dear Bob and Sue,

This morning we checked out of the Evergreen Lodge and drove into Yosemite Valley; it was a perfect day for hiking in the valley. We parked in Curry Village and hiked the Mist Trail up to the top of Vernal Falls. I know you've done this hike many times, and Hannah did it when she was three, but that steep granite stairway with more than 600 steps was a killer. At the top of the falls, we continued on the trail to Clark Point and then back down to Curry Village. The round-trip hike ended up being 6.5 miles. We had heard that the Vernal Falls hike is one of the most popular hikes in Yosemite, but we weren't prepared for the freak show; we saw more than one set of high heels on our way up the granite stairs.

What got me through the hike was my excitement about staying at the Ahwahnee Hotel tonight, the grand daddy of the historic park lodges. Even though it's wildly expensive, we figured it's one of those places we have to experience at least once in our lifetime. Based on what you've told us and the pictures we've seen, we agreed that it's worth the splurge for one night.

Hoping to get the most bang for our buck, we tried to check-in at 1pm. Our room wasn't ready, so we hiked from the Ahwahnee to Mirror Lake, which was a 3.5 mile round trip. The Mirror Lake trail was covered with horseshit and urine puddles to the point of disgust. Did I mention the flies? Having to share a hiking trail with horses is pretty common in the national parks and usually not a problem if you watch where you step. This was more than a nuisance; it was like hiking through a giant litter box. "Leave no trace" apparently doesn't apply to horses. Either the horses need to wear diapers, or someone needs to follow behind and clean up after them. I'm definitely writing a letter to the superintendent.

We were able to check into our room around 4pm. It was a nice room, but I don't think it's where they put the Queen of England when she stayed here. Before we went back downstairs, we thought the other hotel guests would appreciate it if we washed the dust, dirt and horse manure off our legs. Matt went first. When it was my turn, I took off my socks and shoes and stood in the tub in my clothes and turned the faucet on. *Someone* had pulled the little shower knob thingy up, so when I turned the water on, the shower, not the tub faucet, came on full blast. Not only did it scare the shit out of me, it soaked my clothes, my hair and my make-up. Good thing for Matt I started doing yoga, because instead of yelling, I find it's more calming to do deep yoga breathing. I could hear Matt in the bedroom laughing so hard I thought he might stop breathing altogether.

While I was reapplying my makeup, the bathtub was taking a long time to drain, and the dirt, dust and horse manure had turned the remaining stagnant water into a lovely brown soup. I was willing to let it take its sweet time, but Matt said, "There's no way we're paying a million dollars for a room with a bathtub that doesn't drain." He called housekeeping and made a few friends.

We sat in the Solarium before dinner and had cheese and crackers, and beers from our cooler, which wasn't as tacky as you're probably imagining (we left the spray cheese and Saltines at home). Later we ended up eating dinner in the bar instead of the dining room because the dining room has a dress code and we didn't bring nice clothes with us on this trip. For us, a nice restaurant is a gourmet pizza place.

The Ahwahnee dinner dress code is what they call *resort casual* which reads, "Gentlemen are asked to wear collared shirts and long pants, and ladies are asked to wear dresses, skirts or slacks and blouses." This was a red flag for us, not just because they have a dress code, but also because they used words like gentlemen, slacks and blouses. It didn't sound like our kind of place, so we had chili in the bar, which was more like a snack bar than a bar-bar. It had bright lights and kids. After dinner, we sat in the Great Lounge, shared a bottle of wine and read.

Our two observations of the Ahwahnee are: the hotel is

incredible; the price is prohibitive. We're glad we experienced it, but we feel no need to stay here again. We would highly recommend that park visitors spend some time here since they don't have to be a hotel guest to eat in the dining room, hang out in the bar, or sit in the common areas. Next time we're in Yosemite, which hopefully is with you guys, we'll bring books, snacks and beverages, spend some time in front of the massive fireplace, and then head down the road to a hotel that's half the price.

Your Friend,
Karen

From: **Matt Smith**
Subject: **#19 – Kings Canyon National Park**
Date: **September 14, 2010**

Dear Bob and Sue,

Our bill for staying at the Ahwahnee Hotel in Yosemite last night was $521.59. That was just the room charge for a one-night stay. For that price, we decided everything in the room not nailed down was "complimentary." So, expect a package in the mail from us containing pretty much everything in the room that wasn't nailed down; shower cap, sewing kit, two paper coasters, a pen with teeth marks and two pieces of stationary with matching envelopes (sorry one has a coffee stain ring my fault). We wanted you to have these items as our thanks for recommending the Ahwahnee Hotel. We even included the personal note from Priscilla our roomskeeper just in case you want to contact her and ask if there is anything else we could get for our $521.59.

I was going to send you the Bible from the nightstand, but I wasn't sure if that would trigger some form of eternal damnation. It says on the inside cover that it was put in the room by the Gideons. I think they would want you to have it. I asked Karen her opinion. She said, "I have three words for you, do not under any circumstance steal the Bible." She was very convincing, so I hid the Bible in our bag of groceries, and made sure she carried the bag out of the room when we left. As I thought about it more, I realized she was right; it would be wrong to steal a Bible. I'm glad I wasn't the one who took it.

On our drive out of Yosemite, while searching for a granola bar for breakfast, Karen found the Bible under the Tostitos Organic Blue Corn Chips. She was *not* happy. She insists we leave it in our next hotel room. I tried to reason with her, "Why would we leave it in another hotel room? I want to send it to Bob and Sue; they might actually put it to good use."

She said, "No, if we leave it in Fresno then it's like we didn't really steal it, we just moved it, a hundred miles. God will go easier on us."

Who's "us?"

A two-hour drive south of Yosemite Valley put us in Fresno where we turned east and drove another hour to Kings Canyon National Park. Kings was established on October 1, 1890 as General Grant National Park, that date being six days after Sequoia National Park was created. This makes Kings the fourth oldest national park, behind Yosemite (also established on October 1, 1890), Sequoia and Yellowstone (est. 1874). In 1940, General Grant National Park was enlarged and re-named Kings Canyon National Park. Sequoia and Kings Canyon National Parks have distinct areas of land, but the park service manages them as a single entity. Now you know more than you ever wanted about when these parks were established.

Kings has two units. The west unit encompasses the Grant Grove and Redwood Mountain Groves of Sequoia trees. It's much smaller than the unit to the east, which features the park's namesake, Kings Canyon. In 1873, John Muir visited the canyon, and wrote about how similar it was to Yosemite Valley. (By the way, Kings Canyon is more than 8,000 feet deep.) So, we were excited to see the canyon, but an active forest fire was creating heavy smoke along Highway 180, the only way to get there.

Instead of driving into the forest fire, we explored the west unit today. The main attraction in the west unit is the General Grant Grove about a mile from the visitor center. The grove contains the General Grant Tree, which was named after Ulysses S. Grant in 1867. It's the second largest tree in the world right after the General Sherman Tree, which lives just down the road in Sequoia National Park.

The Sequoia trees were stunning. Coastal Redwoods are taller, and Bristlecone Pines live longer, but Sequoias are the largest trees on the planet by total volume. Their most distinguishing feature is a trunk with very little taper. One hundred-eighty feet off the ground General Grant's trunk is still 13 feet in diameter. By comparison their branches look small, but they too are massive; single limbs can grow to be 12 feet in diameter. My camera couldn't capture how massive these trees are; you need to stand at their base and look up to appreciate their size.

Busloads of tourists crowded the paved trail through the Grant Grove. I was standing close to the parking lot with my head stretched skyward looking at an impressive specimen when a woman stood right next to me and began yelling to her friend who was 100 yards down the trail. I shushed her. She looked at me and then began yelling even louder before my shhhhhhhh even ended. It was an impressive display of rudeness. Karen interrupted my deep inhale as I prepared to tell her to shut up. "Making friends are you?" Karen told me that I was not the noise police, which was a shock since this whole time I thought I was. I was outnumbered *and* surrounded; the rude yelling lady on one side and the still pissed off Bible stealer on the other. So I moved on.

Later, Karen and I hiked for several miles in the Redwood Canyon area of the park, also in the west unit. It was a great hike. We saw huge Sequoias, and there were very few other hikers to shush or swear at. Along the trail, we saw massive pinecones. The ranger at the visitor center told us these particular pinecones were from Sugar Pine trees, and they're the largest pinecones in the world. I wanted to put a few in my backpack, but Karen reminded me that it's against the rules to take anything out of the park. I'm married to the enforcer.

We had seen enough large trees for one day, and were anxious to find a new home for the Gideon's Bible, so we drove to the Homewood Suites in Clovis, California (just east of Fresno). We were just in time for their free dinner, beer and wine. It was lasagna night. We also did a couple of loads of laundry. Free food, beer and a washer and dryer that work, we could live here.

Your Friend,
Matt

From: **Karen Smith**
Subject: **#20 Sequoia National Park**
Date: **September 15, 2010**

Dear Bob and Sue,

Matt's OCD flared up today when we visited Sequoia National Park. At home, he's made 58 hanging files, and with his label maker he's neatly labeled each one with the name of a national park. (Yes, he has a label maker. I had one too, in the sixth grade.) He keeps his park files in alphabetic order in his filing cabinet. I'm not allowed to go into his filing cabinet because he says I "won't put anything back where it belongs."

All the stuff we collect in the parks: maps, newsletters, trail descriptions, etc. goes into Matt's park files. He got a little freaked out because Sequoia and Kings Canyon have the same map and newsletter. At the Lodgepole Visitor Center in Sequoia, we were talking to a ranger about hikes in the park when the ranger asked if we needed a copy of the park map and newsletter.

I said, "No, that's OK, we already have them."

Matt corrected me and told the ranger we needed them.

I said, "What? We just got both of them yesterday in Kings."

Matt said, "No, we don't have those anymore. We need the map and newsletter, thank you."

The ranger looked confused and slowly handed him a copy of each.

We moved away from the ranger and Matt said to me, "I have a file for each park, so I need a map and a newsletter to put in the Sequoia file."

"Can't you just put all the stuff from Kings and Sequoia in the same file?"

"I could, but if I needed to find something later which park name would I look under?"

"You could look under both park names, how long would that take?"

"You have a point, but then I would only have 57 files

114

instead of 58, and there are 58 national parks."

"And that's a problem because...?"

"Because, then I would only have 57 files instead of 58, and there are 58 national parks."

I thought for a minute that I was in a scene from the movie *Rain Man.* "And you don't think you have a disorder? That's OC with a capital D."

"No, OCD would be asking the park service to create a separate map and newsletter for Sequoia National Park," he replied.

This is what I live with.

When we get home, I'm going to hide his Lassen Volcanic National Park file and see how long it takes him to notice.

Your Friend,
Karen

From: **Matt Smith**
Subject: **#20 Sequoia National Park**
Date: **September 15, 2010**

Dear Bob and Sue,

It's worth the trip to Sequoia National Park to see the big trees; without the park's protection, they would all be gone. In the 1880s, a group of investors were amassing claims to the land where the Sequoia groves sit today, and building roads into the mountains to carry the logs to the sawmills. They would have cut down every one of the big trees if no one had stopped them. That's why, in October 1890, the park was created, to protect the big trees from being lost forever.

But still, many of the largest trees were cut down, often for foolish reasons. In 1853, a 25-foot diameter Sequoia was leveled to make a *dance floor* to attract tourists. In 1854, a profiteer destroyed a tree named the "Mother of the Forest" by removing its bark, which was then re-assembled as a traveling exhibit.

Not to be outdone in the category of stupid, the U.S. government decided their official exhibit at the 1893 Chicago World's Fair would be made from a section of a Sequoia. They cut down one of the largest Sequoias on the planet, ironically named the General Noble Tree – ironic because it was named after John Noble, the Secretary of the Interior at the time, the guy in charge of protecting America's natural resources – and made an exhibit out of a 30-foot section of its trunk. The exhibit was hollow and had a spiral staircase inside that visitors could climb to the second story. Why did they choose a Sequoia? Because, they wanted to convince the public back east that the big trees existed.

After the World's Fair, the exhibit moved to Washington D.C., but a few decades later it was gone. The government said it was "misplaced" in the 1940s. So to prove a point – that Sequoias exist – they cut down one of the best examples, a tree perhaps 2,000 years old, and within a few decades lost it.

It all sounds like a rant until you stand next to one of these magnificent trees and imagine a jackass with an axe in full backswing.

Today the largest tree in the world is General Sherman; it lives in the Giant Forest a few miles from the Lodgepole Visitor Center in Sequoia National Park. Sherman is nearly 50 feet *shorter* than the Mother of the Forest was when they stripped its bark. Karen and I hiked through the Giant Forest and stood in front of General Sherman. The paved path gives visitors easy access to the big trees, which means it gets crowded in the summer, especially when tour buses fill the parking lot. We took a side hike on the Congress Trail, which was less crowded, and a bit more challenging than the paved path. There we saw other named trees: the Senate, which is a cluster of Sequoias each of impressive size, and the President, a close rival to General Sherman in total volume. If you want to see big trees, Sequoia and Kings Canyon National Parks are the places to see them.

We stayed overnight at the Wuksachi Lodge in the park and ate dinner in their dining room. The food was very good. For our parks trip, this was a rare romantic dinner; the lights were low, there was a tablecloth and a candle on the table. We had appetizers, salad, entree and a shared dessert; we even ordered a bottle of red wine. This wasn't our usual meal of blue corn chips and Coors Light while sitting at a picnic table at the edge of a parking lot.

It was still early after dinner, so we went to the gift store next to the dining room to look around. I was flipping through a book titled *Who Pooped in the Park* when something caught my eye. Next to a bin of chipmunk finger puppets was a display of personalized pocketknives; maybe it was the wine but they fascinated me. What a clever idea, the knives each had a name – Ashley, Brad, Cody – branded on one side and "Sequoia National Park" on the other. There was even an image of a Sequoia tree burnt into the wooden casing. I searched every peg of the display and then made my way to the checkout counter; I laid four knives down. Karen came up behind me when she saw that I was trying to get the salesperson's attention.

"Buying some knives are you?" Karen asked.

"Yes I am."

"What do you have here, a 'Matt', a 'Justin', a 'Bob' and a 'Tammy.' Who is Tammy?"

"That one's for Sue."

"For Sue?"

"I wanted to buy a 'Sue' but the Sue peg was empty. Tammy was the next closest name. I didn't want Sue to feel left out."

Before the salesperson could ring me up, I looked down and Tammy was gone. So was Karen; she was putting Tammy back on her peg.

Bob, look for a package from me in the mail, and tell Sue it's Karen's fault that I didn't get her anything.

Your Friend,
Matt

From: **Matt Smith**
Subject: **#21 – Death Valley National Park**
Date: **September 16, 2010**

Dear Bob and Sue,

There's no easy way to get from Sequoia National Park to Death Valley National Park. As the crow flies, the park boundaries are no more than 30 miles apart. But to get to the visitor center, we had to drive around the south end of the Sierra Nevadas and through the Panamint Range.

After seven hours of driving we reached the park sign at the entrance of Death Valley National Park; it was 2:30pm and the temperature was 82 degrees. We drove into the park from the west on Highway 190. The first few miles were flat and uninteresting, but soon the road in front of us dropped in elevation revealing sweeping views of the Cottonwood Mountains to the east. I was surprised at how beautiful the mountains were. They had no snow and very few trees, but the colors of the exposed rock made them remarkable. We stopped several times to take pictures of the mountains. Unfortunately, it was impossible to capture the dramatic views with my small camera.

By the time we reached the Furnace Creek Visitor Center at 3:50pm, the thermometer on the side of the building had read 111 degrees; the elevation at the visitor center is 196 feet below sea level. We did our park business, but it was too hot to hike. We know September isn't a good time to see the park, so we're planning to come back in the winter when the temperature isn't in the triple digits. Today was just a drive through.

Two and a half hours later we were checking into the Mandalay Bay hotel in Las Vegas where we're spending the night before driving to Zion National Park tomorrow.

The woman at the hotel's registration desk told us the mini-bar items in our room were on a weighted tray. She informed us that if we picked anything up we would automatically be charged for the item.

Just like she had explained, sitting next to the TV in our room was a tray with a cord running out from the back; it was no doubt connected to the hotel's mini-bar inventory control system. From a safe distance, Karen and I leaned over the assortment. We were more interested in how the device worked than what was for sale. I contemplated what would happen if we accidentally bumped something off the tray. What if I tripped on the way to the bathroom in the middle of the night? Would we be leaving here with $378 worth of candy bars, cashews and single-serve screw off bottles of wine? We agreed to stay clear of the tray; all pillow fights, yoga stretches, bad dancing and general flailing around were restricted to the other side of the room.

Karen lingered over the tray. Between the Peanut M&Ms and the stubby can of Pringles was a shiny box with the words "Love Box" printed in red on top. She studied it intently.

I said, "Please don't touch the Love Box. If you do, we're going to be charged for it."

In a belligerent tone, she said, "I'm not going to touch it. Why would I touch it?"

I went into the bathroom to brush my teeth. When I came out, Karen was sitting on the bed holding the Love Box. It was killing her to know what was inside. She shook it, smelled it and even tried to open it, but she was unable to because the box had a safety seal. That makes sense, right? The hotel needs to know when someone has been in the Love Box. I looked at the price list; the Love Box cost $16.80. Karen carefully put it back on the tray. I don't know if the hotel will charge us for the Love Box, but if they do, I want my $8.40 worth of love.

Your Friend,
Matt

From: **Matt Smith**
Subject: **#22 – Zion National Park**
Date: **September 17, 2010**

Dear Bob and Sue,

Springdale got one of Karen's highest ratings for a town: "darling." I don't exactly know what *darling* means, but it makes Karen sound like my grandmother when she says it. Springdale, Utah is a three-hour drive northeast of Las Vegas. When we arrived at noon today, the temperature was in the mid-90s with not a cloud in the sky.

We parked at our hotel and took the free Springdale Shuttle to the Zion Canyon Visitor Center. After taking care of business in the visitor center, we took the park shuttle to the Zion Lodge, a few miles north on the park road. In 1997, the shuttle system was established to eliminate the area's nightmarish traffic and parking problems. The town of Springdale also has a shuttle system. The Springdale Shuttle stops at six locations in Springdale, and the Zion Canyon Shuttle loop stops at eight locations in the park. It's easy to hop on and off either, and the wait is usually never more than five to ten minutes for the next shuttle.

Since we got to the park earlier than planned, we had time to do some hiking. From a shuttle bus stop along the park road, we hiked to the Upper Emerald Pools, and then to The Grotto, about 3.5 miles total. Zion Canyon was an incredible sight today. The contrast of the red sandstone canyon walls against the blue sky and the green vegetation was stunning. The park shuttle took us from The Grotto to the visitor center and from there we walked the couple of miles back to our hotel, checking out dinner options along the way.

Tomorrow we plan on hiking The Narrows, which is a section of the Virgin River that is a slot canyon; an especially narrow canyon where the opposing walls can be as close as 25 to 30 feet from each other. Much of the hike is in the river, which requires more preparation than usual. We need to plan on everything getting wet: clothes, camera, backpack - and everything in the backpack.

The Narrows can only be hiked when the river is low enough to be safe, which usually begins late summer. The gorge is 16 miles long, and in some places, as much as 2,000 feet deep. No permit is required to do the hike the way we are planning to do it, a day hike from the bottom and back. Since it's a slot canyon – there's no place to climb if the water rises quickly – we have to check the weather forecast carefully. Even if it isn't raining in the canyon, a thunderstorm 20 miles away can cause the river to rise dangerously. The forecast for southwestern Utah tomorrow is for clear weather. We should be OK.

There are several outfitters in Springdale whose main business is renting gear for this specific hike: water shoes, water socks and walking sticks. We've spoken with several park rangers about the best footwear for hiking in the river, and they all said that water shoes don't provide enough support for a long hike. They recommended that we wear our hiking boots or thick-tread tennis shoes in the water. We're going to wear the hiking boots we brought with us.

I bought a waterproof Pelican case for my camera at one of the outfitters. I already have a large dry bag to carry our lunch and other stuff that we don't want to get wet. Trekking poles are a must on this hike; we brought our own from home. I think we're ready for The Narrows.

Your Friend,
Matt

From: **Matt Smith**
Subject: **Zion day two - The Narrows hike**
Date: **September 18, 2010**

Dear Bob and Sue,

This morning we didn't get the early start I wanted, but we were early enough to beat the weekend crowd. We took the bus to the farthest stop north in the park, the Temple of Sinawava. Running north from the bus stop is a one-mile paved trail called the Riverside Walk. At the end of that trail is where we started our hike in the river. It was 9:30am and the temperature in the canyon was in the 70s.

Even though all the trail descriptions say that the river *is* the trail, we kept looking for a path. We stood there, at the river's edge, not sure exactly where to go. Pretty soon it dawned on us that there were no choices, the canyon walls at that point were a couple of hundred feet apart. If there had been a trail, we would have seen it. The only direction we could go was up river.

For the first 50 yards, we walked on the bank trying not to get our feet wet. A couple of times we had no choice, so we tiptoed through shallow sections of the river that were a few inches deep. I tried to step past a deep spot and my foot slipped. The water came over the top of my ankle high hiking boots. Wow! The water was cold, even at the end of summer.

I looked up the canyon and saw it was narrower where we were headed. There were places with no riverbank at all. Karen and I looked at each other, and it finally sank in, *the river is the trail.*

There was no use putting it off. I intentionally stepped my other foot into the ankle deep water, and started walking down the center of the stream. Soon, I was knee-deep and struggling to keep my balance. We couldn't have done this hike without our trekking poles.

Looking back at Karen, I could see that she was still negotiating with the river. She was standing in ankle deep water, and looking at the options in front of her. Finally, she followed my lead and waded into the middle of the stream.

Once our shoes were thoroughly soaked, and we were wet up to our knees, we felt a sense of release. We forgot about trying to stay dry, and started enjoying the hike. When we stopped looking down at the river and began looking up at where we were going, we noticed the incredible views.

The light in the canyon was amazing. There was no direct sunlight where we were because of the time of day, and because we were at the bottom of a narrow canyon. Light reached the river by reflecting off the 2,000-foot high canyon walls. The sky reflected off the river; the river reflected light back onto the walls of the canyon. There were infinite shades of color, subtle and dramatic at the same time. The scene in front of us changed from moment to moment. Every bend in the river revealed another stunning view.

My waterproof case was clipped to my backpack at chest level. I was glad I had it. Without it, my camera would have gotten soaked. I was also glad that I brought a dry bag on the hike. Before the hike, I had taken everything out of my backpack, put our essentials in the dry bag and then placed the dry bag in my backpack. Even if I went under, our lunch and extra clothes would stay dry.

We kept making our way up river. There were places where it was too deep and swift to walk through. Fortunately in these spots there was just enough riverbank for us to climb around the deep sections. There were a few spots though where we weren't sure we would be able to make it any farther up river.

At one of these spots I was ahead of Karen. I was trying to find a way forward that didn't involve the river going above my waist. The water was swift and smooth; it tugged at my legs. I couldn't see the river bottom. With my trekking pole, I tested the depth around me. In every direction it seemed deeper than where I stood, including from where I just came. How could that be? The next step brought the river to my waist. I took a deep breath instantly; I had hoped to keep the boys dry for the entire hike. So much for that idea. I took another step, and another deep breath. Easing my hiking boots over what felt like slippery bowling balls,

I secured each foot before lifting a trekking pole off the riverbed. One foot then one pole. I remembered the ranger telling us yesterday, "Keep at least three points firmly planted at all times."

I continued easing my way up the river. Karen was somewhere behind me. I hadn't heard a yelp or scream, so I assumed she was still mostly above water. I began to think that maybe I would make it to a shallow spot without going under. A few more steps and I was dry, standing on a boulder in the middle of the river. I turned toward Karen. She was moving through the waist deep section I had just come through. She almost went down, caught herself, then another near fall. Between wobbles, she looked up at me with a smile and mouthed the words, "I love this."

We hiked about 4.5 miles up the river from where we first entered the water. There was never a point where we had to turn back because the river was impassable, only places where it was challenging to keep from going in over our heads. Neither of us got dunked. We had won a small victory over the river.

While we were still hiking up river, a solo hiker caught up with us. He was soaked and carrying a wooden hiking pole about six feet tall. His backpack was running like a faucet. When he got to within 30 feet of us, he slipped and went completely under the water. Before I could think about helping him his head came up. His mouth was wide-open taking in a big breath. He walked another ten feet and went under again. He'd gotten comfortable with letting the river win; it looked like he had been going under all morning. As he walked passed us, he smiled and said, "How's it going," as if we were passing each other coming out of a Starbucks. He was having a great hike.

The sun was at its highest point about the time we stopped to rest and eat lunch. It was one of the few times on the hike we were in direct sunlight. It felt good after being in the cool water. After lunch, we turned around and started back toward home.

We saw very few people during the hike until we got to within a mile of the Riverside Walk on our return. Being a weekend and a hot sunny day, the river attracted a crowd. What had been a peaceful, secluded hike turned into a crowded noisy scene. This didn't bother us; we had a great hike and were tired and satisfied. All we could think about was plowing through the crowd to get to the bus and back to our hotel room, so we could collapse.

The last quarter mile of the hike was crazy. There were people in the river unprepared to be there. We had sturdy shoes and trekking poles, and *we* almost went under a hundred times. How did these people think they were going to make it up river? Karen almost had a heart attack when we passed a man carrying a baby who looked to be about six-months old. He was holding the baby close to his chest and straining to look over the baby's head to see where to put his foot next to keep from falling. We had to look away and just keep moving. Many, many people were in the river with expensive cameras around their necks. We're sure that at least a few of those cameras went under today.

But the prize for the strangest sight went to the old guy in the middle of the river, water halfway up his legs and with no shoes on, with a walker! Yep, I saw my future right there. Just because you need a walker doesn't mean you can't hike in the river. Good for him.

We rode the bus back to town soaked and sitting butt to butt with people who were dry and wondering where we had been. It felt good to get back to our hotel and into dry clothes. The temperature on my keychain thermometer read 100 degrees. I took our socks and hiking boots and laid them in the sun on the sidewalk outside our room. I pulled the insoles out so they would dry faster. As hot as it was, I thought they would dry enough to be wearable by tomorrow. Forty-five minutes later, they were bone dry, inside and out.

We were too tired to look for a place to eat dinner. Last night we ate carryout pizza in our hotel room. We had plenty left for dinner tonight, but no way to heat it; our room doesn't have a microwave. Karen, without hesitating, took the leftover pizza out of the small refrigerator in our room and went outside. She placed the pizza, still in its foil, on the dashboard of our car and shut the door. After about 15 minutes in the car, the pizza was warm and ready to eat. This is one of the many reasons I married her.

Your Friend,
Matt

From: **Karen Smith**
Subject: **#23 – Bryce Canyon National Park**
Date: **September 19, 2010**

Dear Bob and Sue,

On our way into Bryce Canyon National Park, we stopped to take our picture in front of the park sign like we always do. As Matt took several shots to make sure we got a good one, we heard a crackling sound like a fire. Climbing to the top of a small hill next to the sign we were shocked to see a forest fire burning about 100 yards away. It wasn't a large fire. The burnt area was about the size of a football field. But, it was a fire – in the forest! We hurried to our car to drive to the visitor center and report the fire. Just then, a ranger pulled into the parking area. In a panic, we told him about the fire. He said, "Yeah, thanks, we know about it. We let the little ones burn themselves out."

We drove to the visitor center anyway; we had to get the stamp, buy postcards and change our underwear. Then, we headed over to the Bryce Canyon Amphitheater and got our first look at the hoodoos.

Before this trip, I didn't know about Bryce's hoodoos – incredible sandstone rock formations in the shapes of spires, steeples and castle walls. I've never seen anything like them. We hiked the Navajo/Queens combination loop inside the amphitheater, a total of three miles. It was 70 degrees and sunny, but very windy. The views were spectacular; Matt stopped every minute or so to take pictures.

We hadn't been able to get a reservation at the historic Bryce Canyon Lodge inside the park, so we stayed just outside the park entrance in Bryce Canyon City. Coming from Springdale, which is one of the cutest little towns on the planet, Bryce Canyon City was disappointing.

It's not obvious now, but the "city" has historical roots. In 1916, when tourism around Bryce Canyon was just beginning, Ruby Syrett built a lodge and cabins at this location. Syrett's business, Ruby's Inn, grew rapidly once the area became a national park in 1928. The community of Ruby's Inn officially became Bryce Canyon City in 2007 and the Syrett family still owns the land and businesses. It's a company town; one of the Syretts is both the company's board president and the mayor, a majority of the 138 year-round residents are members of the Syrett family, and nearly all the adult family members are employees of Ruby's Inn or its adjoining properties.

Bryce Canyon City exists solely to provide services for the busloads of park tourists. In addition to the hotel called Ruby's Inn, the city consists of two other hotels, several restaurants, an RV park, a general store, a few fake western shops and outfitters providing horseback rides, ATV tours and scenic flights. It's acres of asphalt, filled with cars and tour busses, fronting both sides of the highway going into the park.

When we asked the hotel desk clerk about a good place to have dinner, he gave us his best sales pitch to buy tickets for Ebenezer's Barn and Grill Cowboy Music Show, located in a building across the hotel parking lot. Tempting, but we picked up sandwiches at the Subway just outside town instead.

Matt thinks it would be a good idea to buy some land just outside Bryce Canyon City, build a hotel and call it *Rudy's* Inn. He thinks we could give Ruby a run for her money. I think he just wants to be the president and the mayor.

Your Friend,
Karen

From: **Matt Smith**
Subject: **#24 – Capitol Reef National Park**
Date: **September 20, 2010**

Dear Bob and Sue,

The first half of our day was spent back in Bryce Canyon. We hiked from Bryce Point to Peekaboo Loop, Navajo Loop, Wall Street and then back to Bryce Point along the Rim Trail. The entire hike was a six mile round trip. Peekaboo Loop gets its name from the small natural arches along the trail that frame views of Hoodoos in the distance. There isn't another place that I can compare to the Bryce Canyon Amphitheater. The colors, the light and the unusual rock formations are one-of-a-kind.

After our morning hike, we drove to the south end of the park and hiked the Bristlecone Loop Trail. Bristlecone pine trees are among the oldest living things on the planet; many are more than 3,000 years old. It's amazing they can live so long in this harsh climate and at such high altitudes (this trail was at 9,100 feet elevation).

We ate our lunch amongst the Bristlecones, and then drove two hours to Capitol Reef National Park just outside Torrey, Utah. Capitol Reef National Park is long and skinny, running mostly north and south for 60 miles. In many places, it's only a few miles wide. One of its main features is the 65-million-year old Waterpocket Fold in the southern half of the park. It's an odd geological formation with a jumble of cliffs and canyons. The park also has many examples of ancient human activity (petroglyphs) and more recent human activity, the abandoned Mormon settlement of Fruita.

We took care of business at the visitor center a few miles inside the park along Highway 24. I was interested in finding out where we could see petroglyphs in the park. There's a clearly marked pull-off along Highway 24 where we could walk to see some, but I wanted to know if there were any others. I asked the ranger at the information desk, "Are there any other petroglyphs in the park besides the ones on Highway 24?"

He said, "Yeah, lots."

"Can you tell us where they are?"

"No."

"You can't tell us where they are?"

"No, I can't."

I think this ranger was more comfortable with trees and rocks than with people. I switched to open ended questions.

"Why can't you tell us where the petroglyphs are?"

"Because people will vandalize them if they know where they are."

That was a fair response. But did we look like the kind of people who would draw boobs and wieners next to ancient petroglyphs? Maybe Karen.

The ranger began to warm up to us. He pulled out a map and showed us where a couple of petroglyph sites were farther down the highway. He said, "I think it's OK to tell you about these." He looked at another ranger standing next to him and said, "Isn't it?" She didn't say a word; she just shook her head quickly back and forth.

"Oh well, you didn't hear it from me."

The area where the visitor center is located is called the Fruita Historic District. It's named after a Mormon settlement that started in 1880. The settlers planted orchards that now have about 2,700 trees. The last residents moved out in 1969, and the National Park Service now maintains the orchards. There was a sign on the desk that read, "Orchards #1 and #18 open 9/20."

"What does that mean, 'Orchards #1 and #18 are open?'" I asked the ranger.

"There are 22 orchards in the park, and when the fruit is ripe they are open to the public for U-pick. It costs a $1 a pound, and you pay by the honor system. Orchards #1 and #18 are apple orchards, and they're open today. Number 8 will be open tomorrow."

After taking care of business in the visitor center, Karen and I picked apples. Well, I picked the apples, and Karen rejected them. She said they had wormholes. I told her that we could eat around the wormholes, but she was worried the worms would still be inside. Instead, she threw the apples to the two deer that were hanging around waiting to eat the ones we dropped. I tried to get Karen to pet one of the deer. She said, "No, they're dirty and probably have deer ticks." She really isn't a big deer fan, unless it's a baby.

In Torrey, we checked into the Best Western. Our room is nothing special but the view out our window is incredible. I suggested to Karen that we go to a different orchard tomorrow and pick apples again. She replied, "God help us". She pointed out that we couldn't possibly eat all the apples I already picked. She said, "You just want to pick apples because it's fun." I had forgotten that we're not here to have fun. Tomorrow we'll hike in the desert instead.

Your Friend,
Matt

From: **Matt Smith**
Subject: **Capitol Reef day two**
Date: **September 21, 2010**

Dear Bob and Sue,

The weather was perfect this morning. It was sunny and in the 60s. We hiked the Chimney Rock loop and Spring Canyon trail in Capitol Reef National Park for a total of 8.5 miles. We didn't see another person on the hike. The canyon was beautiful. The trail was a dry riverbed through a deep canyon with red rock walls. It was obvious that fast moving water had once run through the canyon; the rocks were smoothed over like those from a mountain stream. Some were black volcanic rocks. The contrast of the black and red rocks was striking. It looked like a landscape architect had planned the color scheme in the canyon. We looked for petroglyphs as we hiked but didn't see any.

After the hike, we drove to the roadside petroglyph viewing area along Highway 24. It was an unfortunate example of how people will deface ancient petroglyphs if given the chance. One of the thousand-year old sheep drawn on the rocks had a cartoon voice bubble over its head letting the world know "Amanda luvs Josh." This is why the park rangers won't tell visitors where the petroglyphs are.

Despite Karen's objection to me having fun, we picked apples again today; this time in orchard #8. The apples were better today than yesterday. They were bigger and had no wormholes. There were no deer today, just RVers walking their dogs and watching us try not to fall off the three-legged fruit picking ladders.

We stopped and talked with a couple that lives full-time in their RV. In the summer, they drive all over the country, staying for a week or two at a time in one place then moving on. In the winter, they park their RV in the desert of Arizona along with thousands of other RVers; and hangout in the warmer climate until the weather improves up north. That lifestyle sounds tempting, but I would want to test-drive it for a season or two before selling everything and moving into a house on wheels.

Most people just drive through Capitol Reef National Park. It's difficult to get to many regions of the park because of the park's odd shape. This is not a destination park, but the Fruita Historic District is a welcome relief from the surrounding desert. It has an oasis feel to it with plenty of trees and some nice RV campgrounds. It would be a pleasant place to spend a few days and explore if we had the time, but we don't. Tomorrow we go to Moab.

Your Friend,
Matt

From: **Karen Smith**
Subject: **#25 – Arches National Park**
Date: **September 22, 2010**

Dear Bob and Sue,

Wind and erosion have carved more than 2,000 natural, sandstones arches in Arches National Park. The park service considers any opening larger than three feet in all directions an arch; anything smaller is just a hole. (I know this sounds like something Matt made up, but it's true.) Matt was confused. "They're all holes," he said. "Why are the big holes more important than the small holes? And why do they call a big hole an arch? It's just a hole - that's big."

I said, "Because Big Hole National Park would be a stupid name." That seemed to satisfy him.

This morning, we drove from Torrey to Moab, where we will be visiting both Arches and Canyonlands National Parks over the next four days. We went straight to Arches, five miles north of Moab, and took care of our park business. When we talked to a park ranger about signing up for the ranger-led Fiery Furnace hike, he told us that they were sold out through Friday; and there were only two spots left on Saturday. He said this hike is so popular that it usually fills up weeks in advance, so we were lucky to get the last two reservations.

It was not noon yet, but the sky was turning dark. Rain was on the way, so we decided to do a quick hike to Delicate Arch, which is only a three mile round trip. Towering 80 feet, Delicate Arch is one of the highlights of the park. It's billed as the most beautiful and most photographed arch in the world. It's an icon in Utah; it's even on the Utah state license plates.

We took a short side-trip on the way to Delicate Arch to view a Ute petroglyph panel depicting horses and a bighorn sheep hunt. It was one of the best petroglyph panels we've seen. Someone carved this hunting scene into stone hundreds of years ago, but the bright color of the underlying sandstone was still crisp and clear against the dark surrounding rock. Matt was sure these petroglyphs were made more recently; they looked a little too Disney to be ancient.

Petroglyphs can be dated by measuring the age of the rock varnish on the surface of the carved figures. Rock varnish is darker than the underlying stone and is caused by oxidation of elements in the stone. Once fresh rock is exposed, — like it is when a figure is carved into the stone — new rock varnish begins to form. By measuring the age of the oxidation on the figures, the age of the petroglyph can be determined.

The hike to Delicate Arch was easy, although we got slightly lost for about five minutes. There was a group of older hikers right behind us. We accidentally led them down the wrong trail with us. They thought we knew where we were going. Even though you can *see* the arch from miles away, if you're not careful to follow the cairns, you won't be able to *get* to the arch. We had to backtrack a bit, find the cairn that we had missed, and continue down the correct path. Our followers grumbled. Every few minutes we could hear them behind us asking one another, "Are we sure we're going the right way?" Matt wanted to lead the "geezers" astray again, this time on purpose, for doubting him, but I nixed that idea. I wanted to get to the arch and back to the car before it started raining.

Delicate Arch lives up to its billing; it's a beautiful sight. They say this hike competes with Devil's Garden as the best hike in the Park. We'll be checking out Devil's Garden on Friday.

After the hike, a huge thunderstorm rolled in, so we hung out in Moab and visited art galleries and outfitters. Moab is packed with people; every hotel in the city is sold out. Our hotel desk clerk told us that it's busy like this nine months a year. The city's main industry is outdoor adventure. Everywhere you look there are signs for hot air balloon tours, jeep tours, river rafting, bicycle tours, rock climbing and canyoneering, scenic flights, skydiving and horseback riding. The next adventure we have planned is to navigate the beer menu at the Moab Brewery.

Your Friend,

Karen

From: **Matt Smith**
Subject: **#26 – Canyonlands National Park**
Date: **September 23, 2010**

Dear Bob and Sue,

Canyonlands National Park is near where Aron Ralston got his arm stuck and had to hack it off with a dull knife to free himself and save his life. I assured Karen that if she got her arm stuck today in Canyonlands I wouldn't need to hack; I always carry a knife sharpener in my backpack. There would be no 127 hours wasting away in the desert; we'd be back in time for dinner.

The park is a 45-minute drive from Moab. The Colorado and Green rivers meet in the center of the park forming a "V" shaped plateau. This section of the park is called the "Island in the Sky" because the canyons of the rivers – one to the east and one to the west – have left a high plateau in the center. It's like two Grand Canyons coming together in the middle of the park.

Today we hiked in the Island in the Sky section of the park. After stopping at the visitor center and getting hiking tips from a ranger, we set out at 9:15am on the Lathrop Trail. We hiked from the park road to the rim of the canyon overlooking the Colorado River to the east. It rained heavily yesterday, but today was sunny and in the 60s. When we started our hike, the trail was muddy, but drying quickly. The colors of the vegetation and rocky landscape were brilliant because of the recent rain; it was a spectacular morning.

About an hour into the hike, I noticed hoof prints on the trail. I was taking a picture of the prints right at my feet when I looked up to see a bighorn sheep standing like a statue 20 feet from me. He walked a few more yards away from us, and then stood there for a few seconds staring at Karen and I. Suddenly he snorted, and took off like a shot, running away from us. He must have finally caught our scent. With my camera, I got a good video of him running away. Karen said, "Wow. He's a good runner."

I said, "They're all good runners. The slow ones get eaten."

We kept hiking along the Lathrop Trail expecting to see more wildlife, but we didn't. We saw other fresh prints in the soft, sandy mud that looked like paw prints of a cat – a *big* cat like a mountain lion. I kept imagining that it was following us. We would be easier to bring down than a bighorn sheep.

When we reached the edge of the canyon, the hike dropped a couple of hundred feet below the rim and snaked along the canyon wall. To one side of the trail we could see for dozens of miles to the southeast, following the path of the Colorado River. The morning sun was in our eyes, but the overlook to the river was still amazing. Through my binoculars, I could see Jeeps in the distance driving the backcountry roads down by the river. After a couple of more miles, we turned back. At the car, my GPS said we had hiked 8.5 miles.

Karen didn't like the fact that there wasn't a single flush toilet in this section of the park. The visitor center only had outhouses, and because the smell was overwhelming Karen opted to take care of business outside while we were hiking. She really has come a long way since we started this journey: carrying her own backpack and peeing in the wilderness.

A few miles farther south on the park road (Highway 313), we parked and walked to Mesa Arch. Mesa Arch is one of the most beautiful arches in Utah. I think it's on par with Delicate Arch. We were shocked to see people climbing on top of it: dancing, jumping up and down and posing for pictures in stupid positions. In Arches National Park, the park service doesn't allow people to climb on the arches, but in Canyonlands they do. Not sure why. It's too beautiful a formation to have people crawling all over it.

Mesa Arch was crowded, and many of the people there had traveled a long distance to see this particular arch. They didn't want to wait all day to take a picture of the arch without someone standing on top of it holding his crotch. When the group that had been messing around on top of the arch finally moved on, I started to take a picture. But before I was able to, a woman sat in the middle of the arch to have her picture taken.

No big deal — except she wouldn't leave.

She sat there with her head resting at an angle in her hand while her husband took her picture countless times. Besides the fact that it's just plain wrong to pose for a picture with your head resting in your hands, there were a dozen people waiting to take a quick picture of the arch. The woman could clearly see that she was holding everyone up, but she stayed there and kept changing poses. We gave it ten minutes, and then started back toward the car. Many other people gave up also. I have a message for the park service, "Rope this one off!"

After lunch, we did two more hikes, Upheaval Dome and Murphy Point. In total, we hiked more than 14 miles today. We had extra energy, so we kept going. I like it when we hike that much during the day because then I can eat as much pizza as I want at night. We are going to Zax for dinner.

Back in Moab we had to find a store to buy Aloe Vera for Karen's sunburned legs. She forgot to put sunscreen on them, and they got fried. She called them her "fried chicken legs." That sounds good; maybe tomorrow we'll get fried chicken instead of pizza.

Your Friend,
Matt

From: **Matt Smith**
Subject: **Arches day two – Devil's Garden**
Date: **September 24, 2010**

Dear Bob and Sue,

We woke up today happy that it was Friday, but didn't know why. Every day is Friday for us. But we're still happy it's Friday.

We went back to Arches National Park today to do the eight-mile Devil's Garden hike. The trail leads to eight arches, the farthest being the Double O Arch. The hike got progressively harder as we went. We found ourselves scrambling over slick rocks and walking on narrow ledges that had steep drop-offs. It was very windy, and the wind made parts of the hike even more intimidating.

There was a section of the hike that went over the ridge of a rock formation called a sandstone fin. The initial step onto the fin was only a couple of feet high, but as the trail climbed, the flat surface where we could walk became narrower and the drop-offs on either side became deeper. At a point where the flat top of the fin was only a few feet wide, the drop-offs on either side were a couple of hundred feet. Finally, we had to step from rock to rock to get to the other side of the fin, so we could get back down to level ground. The steps across the rocks were only a couple of feet apart, but it was unnerving because the wind was gusting. We leaned into the wind to keep from being blown off the fin. Had the wind stopped suddenly, we could have fallen in the other direction. We got through that section without any problems, but I find it hard to believe the park service lets anyone do that hike without so much as a permit.

We saw bighorn sheep tracks on the trail, but didn't see any sheep. After seeing the one in Canyonlands yesterday, we keep expecting to see another. You need to be on the trail early for the best wildlife viewing, before the other hikers scare off the animals for the day.

Several miles from the trailhead, we came upon two women

sitting by a small pool of stagnant water that had formed from the recent rains. The pool was about five feet in diameter and was right in the path of the established trail. As we approached the pool, one of the women came up to us and in a nervous tone said, "Watch out for the baby frogs." She directed us a few feet away from the pool, and around to the other side. We could see the tiny frogs hoping around the pool.

A group of six hikers approached quickly from the opposite direction. It took both women to slow them down and keep them from trampling the frogs. Just then, more hikers came from where we had come. The women split up again. This is a popular hike, so I'm pretty sure they spent their entire day racing from side to side trying to keep the frogs from being stepped on. I wondered how long they could keep this up; they looked weary. Surely they weren't planning on coming back day-after-day to protect these baby frogs. Eventually they'll have to give up the cause.

After the Devil's Garden hike, we went looking for petroglyphs around Moab. At the information center in town, we bought a guide to petroglyphs in the area, many of which are not in the park. At the edge of town, across the road from the golf course, we saw several interesting petroglyphs. There was a rock wall not far from the end of someone's driveway with 20 or 30 drawings including *Moab Man*. *Moab Man* is a well-known petroglyph from the Fremont period, which puts it at 600 to 800 years old. It was right by the side of the road. I wonder how many are out in the wilderness that no one knows about.

Your Friend,
Matt

From: **Karen Smith**
Subject: **Arches day three – Fiery Furnace**
Date: **September 25, 2010**

Dear Bob and Sue,

The Fiery Furnace is a twisted maze of canyons where hikers frequently get lost and can't find their way out; the trail is not marked. There are only two ways to hike the Fiery Furnace: with a ranger (strongly recommended) or by purchasing a permit. Most permits are issued to professional guides or hikers who have experience with this hike – like park rangers on their days off. Not wanting to get lost in any place with *fiery* or *furnace* in its name, we signed up for a ranger-led tour. The ranger at the visitor center told us the hike was challenging; it involves scrambling over and sliding down rocks, and passing through squeezes. A squeeze is a canyon so narrow that you can touch both sides of its opposing walls as you squeeze through.

There were 20 of us on the hike today, including our ranger who looked us over carefully and made sure we had followed the pre-hike instructions: sturdy hiking shoes or boots, at least one quart of water each and a backpack to put everything in so our hands would be free to use for climbing. She had us introduce ourselves and tell where we were from. It was interesting that six of the people on the hike were part of a singles RV club and knew one another. How well they knew one another, we didn't care to find out.

Our ranger was a botanist and herbalist. She passionately shared local plant information on our three-hour excursion. At one point, when our group stopped to listen to her tell us about a rare plant next to the trail, I inadvertently stood on a tree root that was growing across the path. Big mistake. The ranger scolded me as if I were 12, and then made an example of me in front of the entire group. She told the group that I had just crushed the blood system of this thousand-year old tree, and may have killed it. Out of the corner of my eye, I could see Matt moving to the back of the crowd. He was trying to distance himself from me. Luckily the ranger hadn't seen me yesterday when I was trying to get the mud off the bottom of my hiking boots by kicking a clump of tree roots over and over.

The three-hour hike was challenging in a fun way. There were several tight spots where we had to press our hands and feet against the opposing walls of the canyon to get up or down the trail. Matt became the designated *extra hand,* helping some of the older women (older than me) in difficult places. It was a snug fit; even on the most open parts of the trail the canyons were narrow. When we stopped to rest we easily lost our bearings; everywhere we looked seemed like the direction we had just come from. Without a guide, we would have been lost for days in there. However, being with a guide doesn't mean you won't get lost. Our ranger told us stories of hikers separating from their group – falling behind to take a photo or to briefly explore a side trail – and needing Search and Rescue to find them.

The scenery was spectacular. The area is named the Fiery Furnace not because it's hot, but because of the brilliant red and orange hues made when the sun hits it in the afternoon and evening. The color and light changed constantly as we snaked through the narrow passages. An occasional tree or bush provided stunning green contrasts against the rocks.

Besides the lecture about not kicking tree roots, we learned some other things from our botanist ranger. (Our favorite was that we should drink gin and tonics in the winter because the flavor for gin comes from juniper berries, which she believes prevents colds.) Also, we met interesting people from around the country who are living life to the fullest. John, an 83-year-old full-time RVer, was climbing over rocks and squeezing through holes like a kid. John was a retired trucker who had driven over a million miles during his career.

We rate this hike a nine out of ten. We had to deduct a point because the ranger did something that never fails to annoy us; she played guessing games with the crowd. As we made our way past countless arches, we played *"Guess what this arch is called."*

She would point to an arch, and each of us had to guess its name.

"Rainbow Arch, Cupid's Arch, Fairy Arch"

"No. It's an animal."

"Elephant Arch, Aardvark Arch, Alligator Arch?"

"No. Look closer. It's two of them, and they're kissing."

"Squirrel Arch (that was my guess), Possum Arch, Orangutan Arch?"

"No... it's Turtle Arch."

Of course it is. Matt was muttering under his breath, "How about you just tell us the name, so we don't have to listen to 19 people calling out stupid answers every time we get to another arch."

After the hike, we ate PB&J sandwiches and hiked to a few more arches. We don't know or care what their names were. By late afternoon, Matt couldn't take any more arch pictures or look up any more arch names; he was arched out.

Moab is a great town for outdoor activities. We should come back here together sometime. You guys would love both parks. Tomorrow is a travel day; we're going to Baker, Nevada and Great Basin National Park.

Your Friend,
Karen

From: **Matt Smith**
Subject: **#27 – Great Basin National Park**
Date: **September 26, 2010**

Dear Bob and Sue,

At the start of every trip, I buy a bag of animal crackers. If there was more nutritional content in them, I could eat nothing but animal crackers for an entire trip. They are my dessert after every meal. Karen won't eat them; she only likes desserts that are "rich and moist." She calls my animal crackers "poor and dry." I like poor and dry. It's a good thing we're near the end of this trip; I'm down to only arms and legs in my animal cracker bag.

Today we drove from Moab, Utah to Baker, Nevada. It was about a five-hour drive. This was the only day we allotted for Great Basin National Park, so we went straight into the visitor center inside the park, which is five miles west of the town of Baker.

When I stamped my passport, it bothered me that the Great Basin passport stamp was larger than the other park stamps. It's a monster. I'm not sure how that's going to look when I frame my entire passport stamp collection at the end of this journey.

We were surprised to see so many people at the visitor center in line to buy cave tour tickets. I didn't know until we got here that the main attraction is Lehman Cave. I told Karen that I wasn't going into a cave unless it was the *only* attraction in the park. Instead, we opted for a hike in the mountains, so we drove to the Wheeler Peak campgrounds at an elevation of 10,000 feet. On the way up, we saw stands of aspen trees with leaves that had already changed to yellow. That was a strange sight, given that only a few days ago we were cooking our hiking boots in 100-degree heat not far from here.

From the campgrounds, we hiked to the ancient Bristlecone Grove. The Bristlecone Pines in this grove are 3,000 years old. The park service knows this because they've taken core samples from the trunks of these trees and counted the rings. The tree that made our Picture of the Day today is 3,200 years old. It's odd that the oldest living plants on earth grow at such high elevation and are buried in snow for much of the year. Even when they're not buried in snow, they're exposed to high winds and a wide range of temperatures. Another mile or so past the Bristlecone Pines, we came to the foot of Rock Glacier, just below Wheeler Peak. It's the only glacier in the state of Nevada. It's not spectacular in size or to look at, but it's a glacier – in Nevada. It was better than being in a cave.

After the glacier hike, we drove out of the mountains and back to Baker where there's a brand new park visitor center. We went inside to see if their passport stamp was *normal* size. It wasn't. I started into a confusing conversation with the ranger about why their stamp was larger than the other park stamps when Karen gave me her "can we go now?" look. Go where? The visitor center was the only entertainment in town.

Baker, Nevada is a tiny town. It's microscopic. Population 68. The motel we are staying at, the Silver Jack, has seven rooms and a stray cat looking for a home. We sat outside, in front the Silver Jack, and drank beers while trying to catch up on email. The motel didn't have a wireless Internet connection, but a restaurant across the street, which had been out-of-business for three months, was still putting out a weak signal that wasn't password protected. In the course of an hour or so, I was able to catch sporadic episodes of signal strong enough to update my email account. By the time we opened our second beer, the stray cat was sitting in Karen's lap. It was staring at her with an "are you my mom?" look on its face. That was not a good sign. I distracted Karen by striking up a conversation with the owner about what was on his dinner menu.

The Silver Jack has a market and a small restaurant/bakery. Thankfully, the food at the restaurant was good since it was the only place to eat in town besides T&D's Restaurant/Lounge/Grocery store across the street. We had pizza for dinner and a slice of sweet potato pumpkin pie for dessert. After dinner, we walked ten feet to the sitting area and sat on a loveseat amongst stacks of books and magazines while checking out the art for sale on the walls.

Karen liked the Silver Jack; she thought it was charming and authentic. She described our room as shabby-chic. I understood the shabby part, but I'm not sure where she saw the chic.

After dinner, we drove back into the park to look at the stars. This is one of the best areas in the country for stargazing. We parked along the road where we sat on the hood of our car and looked up at the Milky Way. It was amazing – no lights, no people, just us and the brilliant stars.

Tomorrow we're planning to drive back to Issaquah, 934 miles. Must get a good night sleep tonight. I think Karen is planning to sneak the cat into the car, so she can take him home with us.

Your Friend,
Matt

From: **Karen Smith**
Subject: **Cannonball!**
Date: **September 27, 2010**

Dear Bob and Sue,

Today was the last day of our current road trip. We had to drive all day to get home from Baker, Nevada. Cannonball!

Since you declined our offer to crisscross the country with us, I thought you might like to know what it's like to be living the dream. A road trip with Matt at the wheel is tiring – for both of us. I made the mistake of saying this to him once. To that he replied, "Really? You're getting tired sitting over there looking out the window, are you? Maybe we should pull off the road and rest until you have enough strength to go on." I think he was joking, but I'm not totally sure.

I started jotting down notes about what it's like to travel with Matt. It's only fair you know these things in case you change your mind, and decide to join us on our next trip.

1. When Matt says "Cannonball!" it means he's not stopping the car until we get there. Of course, we have to stop for gas, so the gas station is where we do all of our business: use the bathroom, stretch our legs, buy snacks and eat all our meals. Shell, Conoco 76, Flying J Travel Plaza – it's fine dining at its best. Matt always says to me, "Get whatever you want."

2. Just as I start to read a book, Matt turns to me and says, "Let's visit." Translated this means, "I'm bored, and you need to entertain me." The problem is, when two people are together 24 hours a day, every day, rarely is there anything new to talk about. There's no point in telling him about my day because he's had the exact same day. No matter what the experience, he probably also saw it, did it, felt it, smelled it. There are times when he turns to me and says, "Let's visit" that my mind goes blank.

3. In our boredom, we resort to playing stupid games. Just north of Jerome, Idaho we smelled onions. We were pretty sure the onion smell wasn't coming from us even though we had been on the road for 23 days. Soon, onions began appearing on the

side of the road. There weren't many, one or two here and one or two there. This went on for a couple of hundred miles; we played Spot the Onion for hours. When we got to Boise, it was raining onionskins. Eventually, ahead of us, we saw the source. It was an open top produce truck filled with onions. Every time it hit a bump a few onions would pop out. Matt finally passed the onion truck, and that was the end of our fun for the day.

4. If I doze off, Matt wakes me because it's my job to keep him awake. He says, "How can you keep me awake if you're asleep?" When I ask him how he would like me to keep him awake, he says, "Let's visit." I've found that scratching his back helps pep him up, but my arm gets tired after about ten seconds. Whenever I stop, he says his back itches more than when I started. He really should let me drive part of the way, so we can each rest while the other drives. When I offer he says, "Not as long as I have feeling left in my legs."

Sound like fun? When would you like to join us? We have some long days of driving in Texas coming up in October. How about it? Cannonball!

Your Friend,
Karen

From: **Matt Smith**
Subject: **Travel day - to Bar Harbor**
Date: **October 11, 2010**

Dear Bob and Sue,

We've been staying at Karen's sister's house in Portland, Maine for the past few days; sleeping on a pullout couch just off the kitchen. Karen's sister has two dogs: a small bug-eyed dog named Henry with a Donald Trump comb-over, and a one-year old German Shepard named Finn who weighs 85 pounds. Finn is an affectionate dog. Every morning he jumped in our bed and bit my ears. This morning after I showered Finn licked my head before I could stop him. All day I smelled like dog spit.

This morning, we drove three hours from Portland to Bar Harbor, where we're staying while we visit Acadia National Park. We ate lunch at a restaurant in town. It wasn't our usual peanut butter and jelly sandwiches out of the back of the car. Today was our "getting the lay of the land day," so instead of hiking we drove through the park along the Park Loop road, around Cadillac Mountain and past Jordan Pond House.

Jordan Pond House is a restaurant inside the park that's famous for its popovers. We ate there years ago, and after having tea and popovers, we bought a special popover pan in their gift shop. We thought we would make popovers every day once we were home. We made them once. I suspect most people who buy the special popover pan have a similar experience. The popover pan never makes it out of the cupboard except for a trip to Goodwill. Karen says Goodwill is the graveyard for popover pans.

After the drive through the park, we ate dinner at a local pub, The Thirsty Whale. Then, we wandered into the Morning Glory Bakery five minutes before their closing time. The woman behind the counter wasn't happy to see us. She was closing shop and had already removed the signs identifying all the baked goods. We pointed to each item one by one and asked what it was. Karen and I each chose a couple of things. When it was time to pay, I asked Karen to fish for change in her purse. I like paying in exact change. Karen always says she has no money, but she can pull endless amounts of change from the bottom of her purse. I paid with six singles, four dimes, two blond hairs and a Tic-Tac.

After the bakery, we walked through town; took a picture of the six-foot lobster in front of the ice cream store, and went back to our hotel. Tomorrow we plan to hike in the park.

Your Friend,
Matt

From: **Matt Smith**
Subject: **#28 – Acadia National Park**
Date: **October 12, 2010**

Dear Bob and Sue,

This morning we woke up to a cloudy day. We struggled to get going. Karen said, "We're like bears; the cooler shorter days are making us want to hibernate." I asked her if she had put on extra weight to make it through the long winter. She didn't appreciate my question. Apparently, she's the only one allowed to compare herself to a bear.

Our plan for the day was to hike to the top of Cadillac Mountain. On the drive to the trailhead, I could sense Karen slipping into a "let's blow off the hike and go for popovers" mood. I knew if I didn't nip this in the bud I would find myself in a Bar Harbor gift store shopping for dishtowels with drawings of lighthouses on them. There would be no popovers, or blueberry fudge, or lobster shaped Christmas ornaments this morning; we were going for a hike.

At 9:30am we parked our car at the Cadillac Mountain trailhead by the Blackwoods campgrounds in Acadia National Park. The lower section of the hike took us through a thick forest. The ground was rocky. Mount Desert Island is mostly a granite outcropping covered with a thin layer of soil. Cadillac Mountain granite is my favorite color of granite, dark red with speckles of black. We saw a lot of it today, of course, hiking to the top of its namesake.

Once we climbed out of the treed section of the trail we started to get better views of the surrounding area. The sun was trying to come out. Occasionally we had good views of the ocean and the portion of the mountain we'd already climbed. Cadillac Mountain is a moderately strenuous hike; it's a 7.5 mile round trip with an elevation gain from sea level of 1,500 feet.

We were both glad we didn't blow off the hike. Since we're trying to visit so many parks in a limited amount of time, we don't have the luxury of waiting for perfect conditions. In

Cuyahoga Valley, we hiked in muggy 90+ degrees. In Glacier Bay, we stood in the rain on the boat tour. In Olympic, we hiked along the beach in a cold fog. We have to show up and do it. Overall we've been lucky with the weather; The Narrows hike in Zion could not have been better.

The second half of the hike up the mountain was mostly on bare granite with short sections passing through trees or bushes. There were only a few people on the trail. When we got to the top, the sun came out as if on cue. We had clear views of the entire south side of the island. It seemed like we were alone in the wilderness, until we were startled by a noise that sounded like a bus. We hiked a few more yards and through the trees saw a sightseeing trolley drive by. There, in the middle of the wilderness, was a parking lot at the top of Cadillac Mountain. A woman strolled past us in gold sequin shoes. She was walking a dog that I doubt could have passed my two-pound test. It had pink bows in its ears. I don't remember seeing them on the hike up the mountain. They probably came on the trolley.

As soon as we started back down the trail, we got the wilderness feeling back. An hour and a half later we were at our car. The morning was a success; we had a great hike, and we didn't buy any useless crap.

With half the day left, we drove to Jordan Pond House and parked so we could walk the carriage roads. The park has 45 miles of carriage roads built by the Rockefellers between 1913 and 1940. John D. Rockefeller, Jr. wanted to travel through Mount Desert Island by horse, so he had the carriage roads constructed as motor-free byways. They are still motor-free today. The roads were carefully planned to follow the gentle contours of the land, so that they disturbed as few trees and hillsides as possible in their construction. There are 17 bridges that are part of the carriage road system. Each is faced with native granite, so that it blends naturally into the landscape. They are beautiful roads; we'll have to come back someday and hike or bike the length of the system.

Today is our last day in Maine. In two days, we fly to Washington D.C. where we will spend a few days with family.

Then on Sunday, we plan to drive to Shenandoah National Park, and spend two nights at Big Meadows Lodge inside the park.

Your Friend,
Matt

From: **Matt Smith**
Subject: **#29 – Shenandoah National Park**
Date: **October 17, 2010**

Dear Bob and Sue,

There were so many motorcycles in Shenandoah National Park today it looked like a Viagra convention. We spent the weekend at my sister Sheila and her husband Carl's house in Arlington, Virginia. This morning, Karen, Sheila and I drove from there to the park. October is a gorgeous time of year to visit Shenandoah; the temperatures are mild, and the trees are in full fall color. The biker crowd certainly thinks so.

After our ritual at the visitor center, we drove to Matthews Arm Campground and hiked to Overall Run Falls. There was a sign at the trailhead clearly indicating no dogs are allowed on the trail. We saw six dogs in the 6.5 miles we hiked. We saw two other dogs that looked liked they weighed less than two pounds, so we didn't include them in the official count.

About a mile into our hike, I heard a loud snap of a branch. I stopped, hoping we would have a wildlife sighting. Karen and Sheila walked slowly toward me looking into the woods. Sheila whispered, "What is it?" I said I heard a sound but didn't know what it was. Sheila said, "I hope it isn't a Saskatchewan." I think she meant Sasquatch, but even so, I assured her there were no large Canadian provinces lurking in the woods.

We've been traveling and staying with family for most of the past 12 days. I've enjoyed it, but it's been tiring. Today, when we got on the trail, it felt good to be hiking. I felt like I was home again.

We drove to Big Meadows Lodge where we had reservations for the night. Wanting to get another hike in before dark, we were anxious about how long it was taking to check in. I could hear the man in front of us talking to the hotel clerk.

"Do them rooms have TVs?"

"Yes they do."

"Them TVs get ball games?"

I wanted to interrupt and say "How would she know if them TVs get ballgames, let's move it along," but with the baseball playoffs and Sunday Night Football on tonight I wanted to hear the answer. She didn't know if them TVs get ballgames.

Our room was in a two-story block of 20 rooms that overlook the valley into West Virginia. Sheila's room was one half of a freestanding cabin with a working fireplace and firewood by the front porch. We put our things in our rooms and went for another hike. The trail beside Sheila's room connected to the Appalachian Trail about 100 yards into the forest. While hiking along the AT, I thought about all the hikers who had successfully through-hiked the entire 2,000 plus miles of the trail, each coming through this very section of trail.

We hiked to the Big Meadow across Skyline Drive then looped back toward the lodge from where we started. A quarter of a mile from the lodge, we saw six deer. Several people had stopped to look at them and take pictures. We stopped also; we didn't want to barrel through the scene scaring off the deer and pissing off the onlookers.

While we were standing there being polite, one of the deer raised up on its hind legs. A moment later, another deer went up on its hind legs. They slapped at each other with their front legs like a couple of kids splashing each other in a pool. Then they stopped and loped off into the trees. I'd never seen anything like that before. I could tell Karen enjoyed this rare wildlife display, but she hid her enjoyment because she had earlier declared she wasn't going to get excited about deer anymore.

We had dinner in the Big Meadows Lodge dining room. Karen and Sheila snuck a bottle of red wine into the restaurant. Their plan was to drink it out of the paper coffee cups they brought from their rooms. Our waiter sniffed out their plan quickly and informed them that guests were not allowed to bring alcohol into the restaurant. They each ordered a glass of wine, and promised the waiter they would keep their wine bottle on the floor next to their purses while we ate. By the end of dinner, the wine bottle was half empty.

After dinner, we walked back to Sheila's room with our half

empty wine bottle and unused paper cups. Outside, a lodge employee on a cigarette break saw us and shouted "You're not going to drink that wine out of those paper cups. Jesus! Stay right there." He dashed into the restaurant. Ten seconds later he returned with three wine glasses saying, "I can't believe you were going to use paper cups." Now that's customer service.

For about an hour, I tried to start a fire in Sheila's cabin. I never got a fire going; the chimney wouldn't draw. Everything in her room smelled like smoke by the time we left and went to bed.

Tomorrow we're spending another day in Shenandoah. Carl is joining us for a hike.

Your Friend,
Matt

From: **Matt Smith**
Subject: **Shenandoah day two**
Date: October 18, 2010

Dear Bob and Sue,

By mid-morning, Carl had joined us, and we were at Fishers Gap Overlook; the start of the four-mile Rose River Loop hike. The weather was mild. It was partly sunny with temperatures in the 50's. A mile into the hike, we met two hikers with a Jack Russell Terrier. They asked if we had seen the bear; we had not. They said they had seen a bear cub, a few minutes earlier, on the section of trail we just hiked. The park's literature says Shenandoah National Park has one of the highest concentrations of black bears in the eastern United States.

About halfway through our morning hike, we passed a group of hikers that included a man who looked to be in his 60's. He was wearing a business suit and black dress shoes. We were at least a couple of miles from the trailhead, but by all appearances, he was enjoying himself as much as the rest of his group. By 12:30pm, we completed our loop by returning to Fishers Gap Overlook; it was lunchtime.

We grabbed the last available picnic table at the Big Meadows wayside. A group of Korean women had an elaborate spread of food laid out across two picnic tables. There was enough food for 20 people. The group consisted of twelve women and one man; he was their bus driver. The women kept hovering around him and putting food on his plate. I caught his eye and he smiled back at me. He knew he had a sweet deal.

Sheila and Carl got to experience our PB&J lunch routine. Carl said he was going "Elvis style" by putting trail mix between his peanut butter and jelly. Carl is on the South Beach Diet. When we had finished our sandwiches, Carl went into the wayside snack shop to "find a restroom". He was gone for 20 minutes. I think I saw him eating an ice cream sandwich behind the bundles of firewood. South Beach can wait until tomorrow; today he was hiking and eating whatever he wanted.

Our afternoon hike was to Rapidan Camp, a 3.8-mile round trip. Rapidan Camp was President Herbert Hoover's presidential summer retreat. Many of the original buildings are gone, but the Prime Minister's Cabin and The Brown House are still intact and maintained by the National Park Service. The Prime Minister's Cabin has interpretive exhibits inside. The Brown House, a few yards away, is only accessible to the public by way of a ranger led tour.

I asked the volunteer ranger why it was named The Brown House. She asked *me* why I thought it was named The Brown House. Rather than saying, "If I knew I would not have asked!" I made a lame guess, so we could move on to the answer. She said, "Well, the President already had a White House, so he named this The Brown House." Yep, I felt stupid for asking.

Her husband, who is also a volunteer ranger, gave us a tour of The Brown House. He did a fantastic job telling us the history of the Hoovers and Rapidan Camp. This was one of the most interesting tours we've taken in the national parks. He explained that Hoover did not accept a salary for being President, and he paid for the land and construction of The Brown House with his own money. After leaving office, Hoover donated The Brown House to the federal government for future Presidents to use as a summer retreat. President Franklin D. Roosevelt, who despised Hoover, did not want anything to do with The Brown House. He persuaded Congress to fund the construction - during the Great Depression - of another presidential retreat. Later, President Eisenhower named the new camp after his son David. Camp David has been the summer retreat for presidents ever since.

We've had a great trip to see the national parks in the northeast, but we're ready to go home. Tomorrow we fly back to Seattle.

Your Friend,
Matt

From: **Matt Smith**
Subject: **Travel day - to El Paso**
Date: **October 26, 2010**

Dear Bob and Sue,

We always get to the airport two hours before our flight
time Today was no exception. (We flew from Seattle to El Paso
to begin a three-park trip to Guadalupe Mountains, Carlsbad
Caverns and Big Bend National Parks.) But even when we're
early for boarding, the process makes me anxious. I worry
someone will cut in front of me out-of-turn; line jumpers should
be shot. Karen adds to my anxiety. She's developed an annoying
medical condition. Whenever she hears the words, "We're ready
to start boarding" she has to use the restroom. I try to get her to
go earlier, but she won't. Her response is always the same, "I
don't have to go."

As Karen returned from the restroom, the gate agent
explained the order of boarding: People with disabilities or in
wheelchairs, people over the age of 100, people who act like
they're over the age of 100, families with children (children are
two-year olds and younger, not fifteen-year olds), in-uniform
military personnel, first class, business class, platinum frequent
flyer members, gold members, silver members, bronze members,
associate members, people who just applied for the airline's
credit card five minutes ago, group 1, groups 2 through 10 in that
order and finally, anyone too clueless to figure out how to get
into one of the groups already called. We had "group 8"
boarding passes. We felt smug pushing our way past the five
remaining passengers who were lower on the boarding list than
us.

I don't like being trapped in a small place, such as an
airplane, with a large cross-section of humanity. I think airlines
should announce before every flight, "Listen up people. We're all
sealed in here together for the next four hours, so try not to be
annoying until the flight is over. Once you exit the plane, *then* you
can whistle, fart, snore, talk baby talk, take your shoes off and

put on as much bad perfume as you want." I think this would make air travel more bearable.

We arrived in El Paso with enough time to pick up the rental car, have dinner (at Carlos and Mickey's) and buy groceries for the week: peanut butter, jelly, bread, water, blue corn chips, peppermint patties, animal crackers and beer.

Tomorrow we're visiting Guadalupe Mountains National Park.

Your Friend,
Matt

From: **Matt Smith**
Subject: **#30 – Guadalupe Mountains National Park**
Date: **October 27, 2010**

Dear Bob and Sue,

Our mornings begin with coffee. Karen and I agreed that, on the road, we would take turns going to the lobby to get coffee and bring it back to our room. "Taking turns" means I will get the coffee every morning in this life, and she will get the coffee in our next life. It's not that she doesn't want to get out of bed; she doesn't want the other guests in the lobby to see her first thing in the morning.

The problem is her hair. Every morning she wakes up with a bump of hair sticking up, always in the same spot. It looks like there's a golf ball hiding in her hair. On mornings when it's her turn to get coffee, she disappears into the bathroom to fix it. She wets it, then brushes it, then re-dries it; sometimes I can smell the hair straightener warming up. While she's fixing the golf ball, I get the coffee.

This morning, fully caffeinated and with flat hair, we drove three hours east from El Paso on Highway 180 to the visitor center in Guadalupe Mountains National Park. The sign at the park entrance warns there's no gas available for 35 miles in either direction. This is a remote park.

When we began our parks trip, there were a handful of national parks I knew nothing about, not even their names. This was one of them. Guadalupe Mountains National Park encompasses the southern edge of the Guadalupe Mountain range, including the highest point of elevation in the state of Texas, Guadalupe Peak at 8,749 feet. The park's stated purpose is, "to preserve the rugged spirit and remote wilderness of the American West." The park is not all mountainous; in the southern region the land transitions from the Guadalupe Mountains to the Chihuahuan Desert.

At the visitor center, we asked the ranger for hiking suggestions. She asked in return, "Do you want a challenging hike or a pretty hike?" I answered, "Challenging." Karen answered, "Pretty." I had wanted to hike to Guadalupe Peak, the main hiking attraction in the park, but I've learned it's a bad idea to force Karen on a strenuous hike she doesn't want to do. We decided to do the pretty hike in McKittrick Canyon.

McKittrick Canyon is in the far northeast section of the park, so we had to drive another 20 minutes to get to the trailhead. For the first 3.5 miles, the trail was flat and followed a trickle of a stream. We hiked past the point most people turn around, where the trail starts to climb in elevation. Another half-mile up the trail, we were high enough to look down into the canyon from where we'd come. Many of the trees in the canyon were changing colors. It *was* a pretty hike.

Before starting back, we took a break for lunch. We spread our butts and backpacks out on rocks a few feet off the trail and ate our PB&J sandwiches. Karen was reading the park brochure while eating. She turned to me and said, "It says here to be careful where you put your hands and feet: watch for cacti, rattlesnakes, scorpions and centipedes." There was a couple of seconds delay, and then we both jumped up and brushed ourselves off. Carefully lifting our backpacks, we made sure there weren't any uninvited stowaways clinging to them. We finished our sandwiches while we hiked back.

October is a pleasant time to visit the park; the temperatures are cool and the colors are changing. On our hike back to the car, Karen kept pointing out the grasshoppers with red wings and the electric blue dragonflies. They fascinated her. I never saw either of them. If she sees them again in Carlsbad Caverns tomorrow, I'll have her checked out – or maybe checked-in.

After leaving the park, we drove north to Carlsbad, New Mexico where we're spending the night. Tomorrow we'll visit Carlsbad Caverns National Park. Guadalupe and Carlsbad are close to each other; the distance between their visitor centers is about 40 miles.

I didn't spend much time checking out the accommodations in Carlsbad before I booked our hotel. I'm hoping we don't have a mouse-on-head, or scorpion-on-head, incident. The welcome card in our room said, "Dear Hotel Guest, Checkout time is 11:00am. The soap, shampoo and shower cap are complimentary. Please feel free to take them. We will charge your credit card if you take any other items from the room: hand towel – $9.99, bath towel – $19.99, washcloth – $5.00, bed pillow – $25.00, decorative pillow – $15.00. If you stain the towels, bedding, or carpet the cleaning charge is $12.99 per stain." That was a nice welcome. *Don't steal or stain or we'll charge you.* We felt welcomed and warned at the same time. Too bad we are only staying one night.

Your Friend,
Matt

From: **Karen Smith**
Subject: **#31 – Carlsbad Caverns National Park**
Date: **October 28, 2010**

Dear Bob and Sue,

I'm 50 years old, and I've never been in a cave, so I had zero expectations of Carlsbad Caverns. I remember hearing about it when I was a kid. It seemed that lots of families would pile into their station wagon, and travel to the caverns. Mine didn't.

We got to the cavern around 9am this morning to take care of business before our ranger-led tour at 10am. A couple of weeks ago, I bought tickets online for the Kings Palace Tour, a 90-minute tour through "four highly decorated chambers." After we looked around the visitor center, and debated whether we should adopt a bat - we decided not to – we picked up our tickets and took the elevator down. There are two ways to get down into the cavern, take the elevator or walk via the natural cave entrance. We took the elevator.

After the 60-second elevator ride down into the cave, the elevator opened into an area with a lunchroom, souvenir stand and restrooms. It was dim down there. The temperature is 56 degrees year round, and very humid. We hung out and talked with the other visitors on our tour while we waited for our ranger to show up.

The Kings Palace tour was unlike anything I've ever seen in my life. Cave experts use terms like stalactites, stalagmites, speleothems, columns, soda straws and helictites for the formations we saw. But I would describe it as a frosty fairyland, a fantasy world that shimmers and sparkles and glitters and glows, a place where gnomes might live. (Matt hates it when I talk like that, so I do it whenever I can.) It was like being in a science fiction movie with the best special effects you could ever imagine. Each chamber we walked through was more elaborate than the one before; I couldn't take it all in.

At one point during the tour, I opened my purse, took out

my mints and put one in my mouth. One of the many rules we were told was that food and beverages are forbidden on cave trails because the smells attract animals into the cave. But something as small as a breath mint isn't considered food, right? Matt saw me do this, leaned over, and whispered, "Right now there's a skunk or raccoon up there that smells your Altoid, and is on his way down."

When our tour was over, we walked through the Big Room, which is the only self-guided tour available. The Big Room Route is a one-mile stroll around the perimeter of the largest room in the cave. It took us about an hour to walk the loop, looking at the highly decorated and famous features including the Bottomless Pit, Giant Dome, Rock of Ages and Painted Grotto.

The park service emphasizes that touching cave formations is prohibited. They are easily broken, and oil from skin can permanently discolor them. I kept seeing these peculiar, white cave formations close to the trail that were smooth and shiny. They appeared to be wet. I held off as long as possible, and then I touched one with the tip of my finger to see if it actually was wet. It wasn't. I know it was wrong to do that, and I felt bad. Matt, who's assumed the role of the park police on this trip, said he was going to turn me in unless I showed sincere remorse. Apparently I did because he let me off with a warning.

Although the park service is meticulous about protecting the caverns, it wasn't always that way. Our tour guide told us that they once let visitors break off cave formations and take them home. Visitors could smoke in the cave until 1955, and for a fee, people used to be able to host events in the cave. In the lunchroom, they used to cook hamburgers and fry chicken for visitors, 800 feet below ground with no ventilation. There's a layer of grease still on the ceiling from that era.

We took the elevator back up and had lunch in the visitor center restaurant. The food was surprisingly good. After we had eaten, we walked down into the cave through the Natural Entrance. From the Natural Entrance to the Big Room, it's a steep, 1.3-mile descent, the equivalent of about 75 stories. The park service recommends that only people in good physical condition access the cavern this way. It was an incredible walk down; we saw the entrance to the Bat Cave, Devil's Spring, the Green Lake Overlook and the Boneyard, a complex maze of partially dissolved limestone rock that looked like Swiss cheese. We also saw Iceberg Rock, a single 200,000-ton boulder that fell from the cave ceiling thousands of years ago.

Seeing the Natural Entrance to the cave really made me admire the first cave explorers from around the turn of the century. Those explorers went down into this unknown black hole with only candlelight to light their way and no paths, paved or otherwise, to walk on. They showed early visitors their discovery by lowering them 170 feet in a two-person bat guano bucket. (Bat guano means bat shit, in case your Spanish is a little rusty.) In 1926, the owners built a 216-step wooden staircase into the cave. A year later, in 1930, the caverns became a national park, and in that same year, the park service installed an elevator.

The rangers encouraged us to stay for the bat flight program at 5:30pm. The program is conducted at the Natural Entrance amphitheater. The bats live in a part of the cave that isn't accessible to the public. Each evening, two million Mexican free-tail bats fly out of the cave at sunset to look for bugs to eat. I guess it's a pretty cool thing to see. Carlsbad Cavern is their summer home, and in late October, the bats migrate to Mexico for the winter, returning to the cavern in April or May. Although the bats were still here last night, the rangers said they would be leaving "any day now." One day, they simply disappear. The crowd gathers for the bat flight program, waiting and waiting, but no bats come out of the cave. We had finished our tours by 2:30pm, and were unsure about sticking around for another three hours, hoping the bats would still be there. I asked the rangers what the odds were the bats would show tonight, but they were unable to give me a guess. What I was hoping for was a bat guarantee. We had a long drive ahead of us, so rather than taking our chances that the bats hadn't already flown the cave, we left for Pecos. That's where we're spending the night on our way down to Big Bend National Park.

Carlsbad Caverns is definitely a place that everyone should

see before they die. It's not just a national park; it's a national treasure. I would love to come back, see the bat flight, and do some of the difficult tours. Of the park's 117 known caves, there are two others, Spider Cave and Slaughter Canyon Cave, which are open to the general public by way of ranger-led tours. I'd also like to see the Hall of the White Giant, where you crawl on your belly, squeeze through narrow passageways and climb slippery, vertical rock. I don't think I'll be able to get Matt to do it with me. He didn't seem to like the cave as much as I did. When you guys come here, please take me with you. I promise not to touch anything.

Your Friend,
Karen

From: **Matt Smith**
Subject: **#31 – Carlsbad Caverns National Park**
Date: **October 28, 2010**

Dear Bob and Sue,

Karen loved Carlsbad Caverns. She would have given it a rating higher than "a magical place" if she had one. I thought it was like touring a dimly lit basement. If I never go in another cave as long as I live, I'd be OK with that. Karen was upset with me because I didn't think the cave was the greatest place I'd ever seen. I told her, "I don't like caves. It's not a choice. I was born this way."

She said, "Please don't write anything bad about Carlsbad Caverns to Bob and Sue."

"You mean, that I thought it was like touring a dimly lit basement?"

"Exactly, please don't say that in your email."

I said, "I'll think about it, but I can't promise." (There are so few things left that I have power over, I'm not giving up creative control of my own emails.)

This morning we arrived at the park with enough time to take care of business and look around the visitor center before our 10am King's Palace Tour in the cave.

Our ranger guide was a young man in his 20s named James. He was very enthusiastic and said he felt privileged to give tours at Carlsbad Caverns. Both his father and grandfather had worked at the park; his father also had been a ranger and gave tours of the cave. It's inspiring when we see a park ranger like James with that level of commitment and excitement toward his job.

James was a great guide, even though he followed the park service standard for giving tours: imagine everyone in your audience is seven years old, don't tell them the answer to a question – make them guess no matter how long it takes - and force them repeat strange words and phrases. We all had to say alunite, speleothems and calcite crust, even though it was obvious most of us had already graduated from the third grade.

But I was a good sport, and did whatever James asked. It's intimidating being 800 feet below the ground, and a mile into a maze of trails; and the 20-something year old in the ranger uniform is the only one who knows the way out. I'll repeat stalagmite and stalactite as many times as he wants if it improves my chances of seeing daylight again.

When the tour ended, Karen wanted to do the self-guided tour of the Big Room section of the cave. She realized that once we got into the elevator to exit, she wouldn't be back. But she was pushing her luck; it was close to lunchtime. I knew there would be no peaceful lunch without first touring the Big Room, so I agreed to the extra tour. I patiently followed Karen, shining my flashlight on the walls every few minutes in fake interest.

The park service tries its best to minimize visitor impact on the cave. Even the smallest contact with the formations can do irreparable damage. They've placed "cave watch" phones throughout the caves, so visitors can report vandalism or bad behavior. The sign on the phone boxes read, "Dial 3030."

I almost had to "3030" Karen. She was fascinated by a particular cave formation close to the path. She examined it from all angles with a goofy look on her face; I knew she wanted to touch it. I said, "If you touch it, I'll have to '3030' you." There was no one else around. She held her finger two inches from the shiny, wet rock for about a minute, like a little kid saying, "I'm not touching it. I'm not touching it." Then she touched it. Maybe it wasn't the thrill she had expected, or maybe she felt bad about breaking the "do not touch" rule, but I could tell she immediately regretted it. I let her off with a warning.

Finally, she turned to me and said in a sad voice, "We should go eat lunch."

We were the only two visitors in the elevator on the way up to the visitor center. The woman operating the elevator gave a speech perfectly timed to the length of the ride. She told us more about the cave, the elevator and the gift store. At the end, she told a joke and pinched my arm. After we exited the elevator, Karen said to me, "That woman was so nice. She's the kind of person you need in a job like that, someone who will make conversation with the visitors."

I said, "It was a script." Karen gave me a scornful look for being cynical.

We ate lunch at a picnic table on the patio outside the cafeteria. It was a beautiful day, just the right temperature and sunny; a perfect day to spend in a hole. After lunch, we walked to the Natural Entrance of the cave. It was an easy half-mile walk. I enjoyed being outside and feeling the sun on my face.

There's a man-made amphitheater with room for a few hundred spectators outside the Natural Entrance where visitors sit to watch the bats fly out each night. A trail from there leads into the cave and eventually to the Big Room where we were before lunch. Karen stood at the lower railing of the amphitheater, staring into the cave like she was watching a party that she wanted to join but couldn't.

It took all my strength to say, "It's still early. Maybe we should hike down the path into the cave for a little way." A few minutes later, we were walking back into the cave. We hiked all the way to the Big Room. Karen didn't touch anything this time, but she still had a goofy look on her face as she stared at the cave formations. An hour of this was all I could take. I had been more than a good husband; I had voluntarily walked back into the cave to make Karen happy when I had already satisfied my companion-for-life duty by being pleasant during our cave session this morning. It was time to get out of the hole.

We took the same elevator as before up to the visitor center. Again, we were the only visitors in the elevator, and the same woman was operating the lift. She spoke the same script. I thought for a moment she was a robot; I wanted to poke her to find out, but that would surely have been a '3030' offense. Each word, pause, wink and pinch of my arm was the same as our first ride up. After we'd exited the elevator, I said to Karen, "That woman was so nice." Karen gave me a scornful look, again.

Back in the visitor center, a ranger encouraged us to stay for the bat flight program at 5:30pm; but it was only 2:30pm. She said last night the bats left early, at 5:15pm. We wanted to know when the bats leave for the season, but she couldn't give us a definitive answer.

Karen asked, "So, you're not 100 percent sure the bats are still here? You can't give me a bat guarantee?"

The ranger replied, "A bat guarantee? No ma'am." The ranger caught my eye and gave me a look as if to say, "I think she may have spent too much time in the cave. You might want to walk her around outside in the fresh air and sunshine." I gave a reassuring nod back.

The timing of the bat migration is largely a mystery; no one knows why the bats leave when they do or where they go. Night after night, from May to October, bats stream out of the cave at dusk to search for insects to eat – moths, dragonflies, and wasps. Two million half-blind bug catchers scour the west Texas Panhandle. Then one night, they don't return. A ranger told us, "One day they're just gone. The crowd gathers for the bat flight program and... no bats. Some years the colony trickles down over a few nights, but it always happens in a very short timeframe." All they know is the bats migrate south. The ranger added, "We don't know where they go, but they return every May."

I find it hard to believe that the park service can't solve this mystery. Somewhere south of here, there's a cave where two million bats suddenly move in, someone must notice. They're Mexican bats, have they asked anyone in Mexico? I can imagine a Mexican National Park ranger telling a group of visitors, "We don't know what day the bats will show up, one day in October they're just here. Some years the colony trickles in over a few days, but it always happens over a very short timeframe."

An attentive third-grader asks, "Where do the bats come from?"

"Well, that's a very good question. We don't know exactly where they come from, somewhere up north."

Of course, if I imagine this conversation taking place in a U.S. National Park the ranger would reply, "Well, that's a very good question. Where do you think they come from?" The third-grader would respond, "If I knew where the bats came from, I wouldn't have asked the question."

Someone out there knows where the bats go. The park service needs to find that person, and ask them to notify Carlsbad Caverns. It's a simple phone call once a year to say, "The bats are here now; you can stop the bat flight programs."

Unable to get a bat guarantee, we left the park and drove to Pecos, Texas where we're spending the night. (We're on our way to Big Bend National Park.) I think we made the right decision not to wait for the bat flight program. The drive to Pecos took longer than we thought, and we lost an hour due to changing time zones.

I have a feeling we haven't seen the last of Carlsbad Caverns. Karen told me that she wants to go back and tour Spider Cave and Slaughter Canyon. Who comes up with these names? Spider Cave? If I didn't want to go into a regular cave, what makes her think I would want to go into a cave with spiders? I told her, "Yeah, that's sounds great. Maybe we could tour Put Your Scrotum in a Vise Cave while we're at it."

Your Friend,
Matt

From: **Matt Smith**
Subject: **#32 – Big Bend National Park**
Date: **October 29, 2010**

Dear Bob and Sue,

We left Pecos early this morning on our way to Big Bend National Park. There wasn't much to see on the drive. The towns kept getting smaller the farther south we went. Many of them looked deserted with buildings falling down. Karen rested her head on her hand while staring out the window. Every time we went through one of these towns she would mumble, "Ramshackle." About an hour north of the park, we came to Marathon, Texas. Karen said it was a "cute little town." That's just below "darling" on her rating scale, but still a decent rating.

Marathon has a few art galleries, a nice town center and what appeared to be some interesting places to eat. It was too early for lunch, so we stopped only long enough for gas.

Big Bend National Park is mostly desert with the Rio Grande as its southern border. Sitting in the middle of the park is an area of mountains – the Chisos Mountains. That's where we are staying for the next couple of nights, at the Chisos Mountain Lodge. A paving crew was resurfacing the road to the lodge, so we spent the day in the other areas of the park until they finished.

We took care of our business at the Panther Junction Visitor Center - where I expected to see a panther but didn't - then drove to the Boquillas Canyon Trail parking lot in the southeast corner of the park. The Rio Grande cuts through Boquillas Canyon, and there is a short trail leading to the east from the parking lot on the U.S. side of the river. The park newsletter warns against buying anything from Mexican Nationals, and against crossing the border (Rio Grande) in any direction. Before 9/11, the border was open, but, "As a result of a 2002 US Customs and Border decision, there are NO authorized border crossings anywhere in the park."

Along the short hike from the parking lot to the riverbank,

souvenirs sat displayed on rocks. Handwritten cardboard signs with prices for the souvenirs leaned against collection jars. These were items made by Mexican Nationals. They cross the river in small boats, place their items next to the trail for U.S. tourists to buy, and then go back across the river to Mexico and wait for customers. As soon as Karen stopped to look at a display of beaded wire scorpions, we heard someone yelling from the other side of the river. It was a guy sitting on the bank watching his merchandise. We think he was shouting his encouragement for us to buy something, but we didn't.

Farther down the trail, we came to the sandy bank of the Rio Grande where a man was standing on the U.S. side next to a tip jar singing "La Cucaracha." His voice rang off the canyon walls. We kept moving along the trail without slowing down.

There was a man and a woman hiking ahead of us on the trail. It didn't take us long to pass them. This is what we do; the goal of every hike is to pass the people in front of us. Karen doesn't like passing people because she has to increase her speed when she's already going faster than she would like. She says to me, "It's not a race." But she's wrong; it *is* a race.

When we passed the couple, we saw they were older than us, maybe 65ish. They had covered every inch of their bodies with clothing, except their faces. It was a hot day, but they were wearing gloves. They even had reflective straps pulled tight around the cuffs of their pants. I'm guessing to keep out dust or bugs, but I'm not sure why. They looked like a HAZMAT team. A few hundred yards later, the trail ended, so we turned around and headed back toward the car. Just then, I saw a head floating in the river. It was the man we had just passed on the trail. He had gone to the edge of the river, taken off all his clothes except his briefs and was swimming across the river. Only his head was above the water. His wife, still in her HAZMAT suit was standing on the shore filming him.

The river's current was swift. I was concerned he wouldn't make it across, and even more concerned that I'd have to jump in and save him. He climbed out on the Mexican side of the river, and jumped up and down waving his arms for the camera.

I'm not sure how he planned on getting back. I couldn't see a safe place where he could make it back across. We didn't want to interfere with (or witness) any more of this odd behavior, so we continued hiking toward our car. He must not have read the park warnings about it being illegal to swim across to Mexico, or the health hazards of swimming in the river. The park newsletter advises against swimming in the Rio Grande because, "Water-borne micro-organisms and other waste material can occur in the river and cause serious illness." It's a sewer.

At the car, we ate our PB&J sandwiches, but still had hours to kill, so we drove several miles down a gravel road to the Grapevine Hill trailhead, and hiked to Balanced Rock. It was an uneventful hike, but we enjoyed hiking in the desert and getting the exercise. After an hour of hiking, we reached the balanced rock. Karen posed for a picture standing in front of the rock with her arms up, making the picture look as if she was holding the rock above her head. This is what we quit our jobs to do, take silly pictures of us in the middle of nowhere. Well, it's better than working.

The road to the lodge opened, and by dinnertime, we were checked-in to our room. The Chisos Mountain region is different from the rest of the park; it's higher in elevation at 5,000 feet, it's cooler by about five to ten degrees and it's mostly treed. Tomorrow we plan on hiking in the mountains.

Your Friend,
Matt

From: **Matt Smith**
Subject: **Big Bend day two**
Date: **October 30, 2010**

Dear Bob and Sue,

This morning we hiked the Lost Mine Trail in the Chisos Mountains, a 4.6-mile round trip. There was not a cloud in the sky; temperatures were mild and we could see for miles into Mexico from the top of the trail. We were half hoping we'd see a mountain lion on our hike this morning, and half hoping we wouldn't. They live in this section of the park. I've read stories of visitors seeing them walk through the parking lot of the Chisos Basin Visitor Center. We didn't see a mountain lion today. But, it's likely a mountain lion saw us.

After the hike, we had lunch at the trailhead parking lot: PB&J sandwiches and animal crackers – again. When we arrived in El Paso earlier this week, I bought a 48-ounce bag of animal crackers for $2.99. While putting them in the car, the bag burst open and all the animals spilled onto the seat of the car. We've been driving around with an open mound of animal crackers in the back. All week I've been eating off the mound, but it doesn't look to be getting smaller. Karen is concerned to see me eat something that has touched the seat of a rental car because that's not like me. Normally I wouldn't, but it's a big pile; a 48-ounce bag is a lot of animal crackers. The ones on the top haven't touched the seat. I'll have to decide when I get to the bottom of the pile if I'll eat the ones that have come in contact with the seat where someone's butt rested. Probably not.

In the afternoon, we hiked The Window trail, which was a 5.6 mile round trip according to my GPS. The trail begins at the Chisos Mountain Lodge parking lot. It follows a dry wash that only runs after heavy rains. The end of the trail (the window) is a 200-foot drop that becomes a pour-off (waterfall) when the stream is running. At dusk, the window frames the sun setting over the desert below.

I need to add a leash for Karen, the shoulder harness type

that parents use for hyperactive toddlers, to my list of things to carry in my backpack. Karen likes to walk to the edge of cliffs, ledges and drop-offs, and lean over to get a view of what's below. I'm worried that one time she's going to disappear over the edge. That would be bad; the AAA membership is in her name.

After the hike, Karen and I sat at a picnic table in the shade next to the visitor center. We connected to the lodge's wireless; read our email, and connected to the Internet, so we could check the status of Hurricane Tomas. If the current forecast holds true, we will meet Tomas in two weeks at Virgin Islands National Park.

Five deer snuck up behind us while we were sitting there. We kept hearing people yelling from the deck of the restaurant, "Look behind you." When we turned around we could see that one of the deer was clearly smaller than the others. Karen has a soft spot for runts. I have nothing against runts, but I told her not to get too attached; mountain lions target the small ones. She didn't want to believe this. Later four deer came by. I don't know if they were the same group as before, but Karen was concerned there wasn't a little one with them. She kept looking around the parking lot for number five.

We had dinner at the lodge, and then went back to our room and ate a bag of candy corn that I bought at a gas station yesterday. We don't know what's in candy corn, but neither of us could stop eating it. It must have an ingredient that's addictive. Twenty years from now, an investigative reporter is going to find a secret candy corn company memo that proves they've known this the whole time. It'll be on *60 Minutes*.

Your Friend,
Matt

From: **Karen Smith**
Subject: **Happy Halloween**
Date: **October 31, 2010**

Dear Bob and Sue,

To celebrate Halloween, Matt and I dressed up like unemployed, middle-aged, don't-know-what-to-do-with-the-rest-of-our-lives hikers. The ranger at the visitor center said our costumes were spot on.

We spent today on the west side of Big Bend National Park. Our first activity was hiking the Upper Burro Mesa Pouroff trail; it was a 3.6 mile round trip. The first half-mile of the trail was across open desert, and then it descended through a narrow, rocky gorge to the upper lip of a waterfall. (It wasn't a waterfall when we were there. It's a waterfall only after a heavy rain.) Centuries of floodwaters carved a sandy pothole cave at the end of the hike where a narrow slot in the cave wall forms the top of the 100-foot pouroff. It was an amazing hike.

For our second hike of the day, we took the ranger's suggestion and hiked the Chimneys Trail, which was a few miles south of our first hike. From the trailhead of the Chimneys Trail, you can see across the desert floor to the turnaround point for this hike; a row of rock outcroppings called the chimneys. Unless a hike itself is outstanding, like The Narrows or a slot canyon, I like it when there's a reward at the end. Something to look forward to, like a waterfall. It keeps me going when Matt is on his death march.

The hike *to* the chimneys was not particularly interesting, but the ranger told us that Indians once lived near the chimney rocks and left petroglyphs there.

Once we reached the Chimneys; smaller trails fanned out between and around the formations. We found the petroglyphs carved on the flat stone surfaces along the base of one of the pinnacles. This hike ended up being a five mile round trip; on our way back we were baking like potatoes in the afternoon desert sun. The trail was all ours; we saw no one else the entire time.

Blasting the car's air conditioning, we drove to the Castolon Historic District in the southwest part of the park, a farming and ranching area from the early 1900's to the 1960's. We went to the visitor center and The La Harmonia Company Store. The store has been in operation for more than 90 years, now catering to tourists instead of farmers and ranchers. In addition to the store, Castolon includes the oldest known adobe structure in Big Bend National Park (the Alvino House), another store building (the Old Castolon) and numerous adobe ruins that were once homes for the Mexican American and Anglo families that lived in the area.

We drove the short distance from the visitor center to Santa Elena Canyon. Along the way, we pulled off the road and hiked one mile to Dorgan House, which is a spectacular adobe ruin, formerly the home of Albert Dorgan. It was a working ranch house in the early part of the 20th century, but abandoned when the park service took the area over in 1944. The chimney is still largely intact and is made entirely of petrified wood found in the area. That alone was worth the one-mile hike.

At Santa Elena Canyon, we walked down to the edge of the Rio Grande, one of the most famous scenic features of Big Bend. There, the Rio Grande cuts a 1,500' vertical chasm out of limestone. The left wall of the canyon is in Mexico, and the right is in Texas. They say floating through the canyon is a spectacular adventure, but once Matt got a close up view of the brown water, the chance of us ever doing that evaporated.

Our last stop of the day was Terlingua, Texas just outside the park. Terlingua has a few hotels, several restaurants and a couple of float-trip outfitters. It's another former mining town that was deserted after its mining operations ceased. During the late 1960s and early 1970s, tourism overflow from the park brought new life to the town. Terlingua became famous for its annual chili cook-off, and in 1967 was deemed the "Chili Capital of the World". The cook-off is always held on the first Saturday in November, so it looks as though we'll miss it by six days.

A park ranger we met in Glacier Bay, who once was a

ranger at Big Bend, recommended that we stop at Long Draw Pizza for dinner. But when we got there at 5pm, they weren't open yet. We found a restaurant down the road in the El Dorado Hotel, and ate nachos at the bar while we waited for Long Draw to open. The El Dorado was clearly a family-run place. There were two young Hispanic girls sitting at a table behind us doing their homework. They spoke Spanish to their mom who was tending bar. The mom told me her daughters were asking her what my name was and where I came from. I turned around and chatted with the girls for a bit. They couldn't wait to go trick-or-treating. They were adorable.

For Matt and I, an unexpected and wonderful bonus of this parks trip has been the opportunity to visit the small towns near the parks, try the local cuisine and meet the people who live there.

We headed back to the pizza place, which didn't look very promising from the outside; it's a weathered trailer in a gravel parking lot. There were quite a few people inside, which is usually a good sign for a restaurant. We sat at the bar, talking to the owner Nancy while she made our pizza. We've had countless pizzas on our parks trip, and Long Draw Pizza was one of the best.

I mentioned to Matt that I'm not sure we've eaten a vegetable in five months, unless we consider tomato sauce on pizza a vegetable. He pointed out that beer is plant-based, so it counts as a vegetable, and assured me that we're getting all the nutrients we need.

Nancy encouraged us to stay for their Halloween party. She was expecting the place to "get crazy" later on, but since we can't stay up past 9pm we declined. We finished our pizza and were out of there by 7pm. Tonight we have to pack and get ready for our flight home tomorrow from El Paso. Hope you're having a fun Halloween. Bob, maybe by next year we'll have that park ranger uniform for you to wear.

Your Friend,
Karen

From: **Matt Smith**
Subject: **#33 – Virgin Islands National Park**
Date: **November 9, 2010**

Dear Bob and Sue,

We're pressing our luck trying to save a few dollars by visiting the Virgin Islands during hurricane season. Today, heavy thunderstorms, remnants of hurricane Tomas, caused our flight from Miami to St. Thomas to be diverted to Puerto Rico. The plane sat on the tarmac in San Juan for a couple of hours before the weather improved enough to continue.

Yesterday we began a four-park trip to the Virgin Islands and Florida. The first park we're visiting is Virgin Islands National Park, on the island of St. John. There's no large airport on St. John, so we had to fly to St. Thomas, and then take a shuttle bus and ferry the rest of the way.

We were already late getting into St. Thomas, and the shuttle bus ride from the airport to the ferry terminal took an hour because of slow traffic. The trip was turning into a grind. So, I was relieved when the guy sitting next to me on the shuttle bus talked on his cell phone the entire time. Karen was on one side of me, and cell phone guy was on the other. I was trapped.

He was explaining to the person on the other end of the phone how he and his family had just run the New York Marathon, and were spending the week on St. John as their reward. In case you're wondering, the last hour and a half of the marathon was torture for him; it was all he could do to keep putting one foot in front of the other. Now he's dealing with blisters on both heals and losing his toenails because the race was so hard on his feet. That's nice.

It had been a long day and a half of travel, so we very much appreciated the Painkillers they served us on the ferry. A Painkiller is a local drink made with rum, fruit juice and coconut.

The ferry took us directly to Caneel Bay Resort, where we're staying the next three nights. As we pulled up to the dock, the resort staff greeted us. A staff member drove us to our room in a golf cart, gave us our keys and left. When we stepped inside, we noticed a small problem with our room; everything was wet. Not damp, wet. The welcome card from the hotel, the tile floor, the bed sheets, the pillows and the towels were all wet. The ceiling dripped. We went to the front desk and told them that our room had flooded; we couldn't imagine what else could have happened. The front desk clerk said, "We'll send someone to your room to mop the water off the floor." I said, "No it's not just the floor, everything in the room is wet." He said, "Sir, all the rooms are like that, it's very humid here."

We ate dinner at the outdoor grill. The food and service were excellent, but the noise coming from the surrounding jungle was so loud we could barely hear each other speak. Karen described it as an, "Eeeeee! Eeeeee! Eeeeee!" shriek. She asked our waiter what the noise was. He said, "Creeckeets."

Karen said, "Creeckeets? Is that a type of monkey?"

I interrupted, "He said *crickets*. Those aren't monkeys. Where do you think we are?"

The waiter looked confused, "No monkey, is creeckeets."

After dinner, we walked back to our room in the darkness using the small flashlights the hotel gave us at check-in. Karen was shining hers in the trees looking for monkeys.

Your Friend,
Matt

From: **Matt Smith**
Subject: **Virgin Islands day two**
Date: **November 10, 2010**

Dear Bob and Sue,

Before going to bed last night, I put all my stuff in the dresser to keep it from getting wet. Condensation was dripping from the ceiling, and I was concerned that I'd wake up and not have any dry clothes, or worse, that my phone and my camera would be wet. We cranked the air conditioner to suck the humidity out of our room. I shivered all night. At four in the morning, the sheets on my side of the bed were finally dry enough that I could fall asleep.

Walking to breakfast we saw deer on the property lawn, but no donkeys. We had read there are wild donkeys on the island. Yesterday the resort manager told us that donkeys occasionally wander onto the property, but this week they're in a corral on the other side of the island. How wild could they be if they're in a corral?

We ate breakfast at the hotel's open-air restaurant. Like last night, the food and service were exceptional. We had to move several feet away from the roofline because it began to rain on us. As we ate, the rain got heavier. There are two paths to take when the weather is miserable; we can hunker down in our room and try not to kill each other until the weather improves, or we can go out in it and act as if we're having fun. Today we hiked in the rain.

I stuffed extra shirts for Karen and me in my dry-bag along with everything else I wanted on the hike: phone, camera, wallet, etc. The dry-bag went into my backpack a la The Narrows hike. The plan was to hike from Caneel Bay Resort through the park to the visitor center, a mile and a half through dense vegetation. (It was a jungle.) The visitor center is on the edge of the small waterside town of Cruz Bay. We wore flip-flops despite the hotel staff's recommendation against it. Two Caneel Bay umbrellas from the front desk completed our outfits.

On the hike, the rain never let up. The trail to the visitor center was a flowing stream. We hiked in flip-flops through ankle high water. The umbrellas kept some of the rain off of us when they weren't turned inside out because of the wind. It was one of the most enjoyable hikes of our parks trip. The temperature was warm, and the rain was invigorating. We were out doing it and having fun. It was much better than sitting in our hotel room trying to decide which personality traits we dislike the most about each other.

We were the only visitors in the visitor center. After stamping my passport, I double bagged it in sandwich bags before putting it back in the dry-bag. It's not likely we will ever be at this visitor center again, and I didn't want my passport stamp to get wet.

The ranger at the visitor center didn't say much. Usually I'm the quiet one in a conversation, but when I find someone less talkative than me, I turn into question guy. Coming from Chicago ten years ago, he's been a park ranger here ever since. He's concerned that the park "might not make it." He told us that one of the conditions the Rockefellers attached to their donation of this land to the federal government was that if it ever fails to be a national park, the ownership would revert to the Rockefeller family. (In 1956, they donated a little more than half the island of St. John to the federal government, so it could be made into a national park.) With low visitors numbers and federal budget cuts, he's concerned the park might fail. We don't know if this is possible, but he seemed genuinely worried about it.

When the rain lightened, I set my camera on a tiny tripod in a puddle and took our picture in front of the park sign. Then, we walked two blocks to the center of town, but there wasn't much going on in Cruz Bay. At an open-air bar, we sat and had a snack then walked around the small town. Last night Karen found the recipe for Painkillers in a magazine; it calls for orange juice, pineapple juice, rum and Coco Lopez. Karen had taken to-go cups of orange juice and pineapple juice from the breakfast buffet this morning in anticipation of making her own Painkillers this afternoon. Normally Karen doesn't do carry-out from buffets but when she saw the bill for our room package she figured everything was fair game. (She may have also brought the toaster back to our room.)

With the bottle of complimentary rum in our room, and the juice from the breakfast buffet, the only missing ingredient was Coco Lopez. Before hiking back to the resort, we went to a convenience store to look for Coco Lopez. Jackpot! We bought a bag of blue corn chips, two coconut long boys and a can of Coco Lopez. (A coconut long boy is a chewy candy made from what appears to be low-grade motor oil and shredded coconut. I ate one and put the other in my backpack.)

The hike back to the resort was the same as before: rain, wind, inside-out umbrellas and ankle-deep water. It was enjoyable, just as before, except we both got blisters from hiking in flip-flops. In the afternoon, we drank Painkillers until we could no longer feel the blisters.

Tonight we wanted to walk along the road into town for dinner, but the hotel staff strongly recommended against it; there are no streetlights, sidewalks, or shoulders to walk on, just a narrow road with jungle on both sides. We took their advice and hired a cab. The cabs here are pickup trucks with bench seats in the bed and a canopy over the top. The drivers go very fast on pitch-black curvy roads. It was a good thing we had Painkillers before we climbed in the back of the cab; they kept us relaxed during the wild ride. Otherwise, we would have jumped out and into the jungle after a couple of blocks. Fortunately, it was not a long ride into town.

Dinner in Cruz Bay was casual: burgers and beers. Hanging out in a locals' restaurant is more our style than an expensive dinner at the resort. After dinner, we strolled through town several times then caught a cab back to Caneel Bay. It was still early when we returned, so we walked back and forth along the short beach in front of the resort until we'd stretched our legs enough for one day. Tomorrow, if the weather improves, we're going to the beach.

Your Friend,
Matt

From: **Matt Smith**
Subject: **We have a new best friend**
Date: **November 11, 2010**

Dear Bob and Sue,

Karen woke up with diaper rash. I didn't get any more details than that from her. I had my own problems; the zipper on my shorts had rusted in the down position.

At breakfast, we did our best to eat our weight in food. I'm pretty sure I ate a pound of bacon alone; I was thirsty all day. We took as much orange and pineapple juice from the buffet as we could carry. Karen had a bagel hanging out of each pocket. We were no longer trying to be discreet. Karen said, "If they don't like it they know where to find us, in the room with the dripping ceiling."

By mid-morning, the weather had cleared. We found ourselves at the beach lying on lounge chairs. There are several beaches on the Caneel Bay property. The one we landed on was perfect; it was secluded with clean, smooth sand and calm waves. We pulled our lounge chairs under the trees at the edge of the beach and enjoyed just being there.

Inflatable rafts were stacked in a pile. I grabbed a couple and dragged them to our spot. We alternated from lounging on our chairs to floating on the rafts. I floated belly down on my raft with my face in the water, lazy man snorkeling. When I got tired of paddling I let the waves carry my raft onto the beach. I wouldn't move until the raft came to a complete stop on the sand. Then, I'd lie on my lounge chair for 20 minutes and repeat the cycle. This went on all day.

Normally I wear sunscreen, but today it seemed like too much effort. Deciding to go native, I declared it a sunscreen holiday. I thought the hair on my back and stomach would be at least an SPF 15. Nope, I got fried. But not to worry, we had something to kill the pain. Every hour or so, I would trek back to our room, make Painkillers and bring them to the beach. Each time the ceiling dripped into one of the cups, I would make that one Karen's drink.

On one of my Painkiller runs, I saw a large iguana on the lawn. I set the drinks in the grass and took its picture. I didn't know if it was a biter, so I kept my distance. But, I must have gotten too close regardless because he flared his neck thing, so I backed off. It was time to move on to the beach anyway; bugs were jumping into Karen's Painkiller.

I could have saved time and long walks by ordering from the drink cart guy, but it was cheaper for me to make the drinks myself. I didn't realize how much cheaper, until in a moment of weakness, I ordered two Painkillers from him. While I watched him make the drinks, I was thinking that I could be doing this myself for free in our room. The only difference; he charged me $20!

Back at the beach I nudged Karen out of her sun/rum coma. She took one sip of her new drink, turned to me and said, "I've decided that we are going to dedicate our lives to the coconut." There was a pause. "No wait, the coconut is going to dedicate its life to us." It's at times like these I've found it best just to listen and let the wisdom flow without interruption. She continued, "The coconut represents everything that is good in the world; the way it smells, the way it tastes, you can rub it on your body, you can eat it, you can drink it, it relaxes you, it represents the vacation lifestyle." I looked at her in awe. She was silent for a while looking out over the ocean. Then she asked with surprising urgency, "Is it a fruit or a nut?"

Later there was some discussion about how we could enforce the declaration that the coconut would dedicate its life to us. We agreed we needed to work out some of the finer details, but otherwise it was a sound plan.

Bob and Sue, I hate to break this to you in an email, but we have a new best friend, and his name is Coco Lopez.

Your Friend,
Matt

The End of Volume One

Thank you for sharing this journey with us. *Dear Bob and Sue Volume One: Into the National Parks* is intended to be the first in a series of books about our trips to the national parks. Please look for other volumes in this series.

Matt and Karen Smith

We encourage and welcome your feedback.

Email us: dearbobandsue@gmail.com
Follow us on Facebook:
http://www.facebook.com/dearbobands
Visit our website: http://www.dearbobandsue.com

ABOUT THE AUTHORS

Matt and Karen Smith have been married for 30 years. They were born and raised in the Midwest but now make their home in Issaquah, WA. Matt has worked in the financial services industry for his entire career. In addition to his travel writing, he has authored several finance books published by John Wiley & Sons. *Dear Bob and Sue* is his first published work intended for a general audience. Matt and Karen have three grown children and a son-in-law.

Made in the USA
Lexington, KY
15 May 2012